fusion

fusion

TURNING FIRST-TIME GUESTS INTO
FULLY ENGAGED MEMBERS OF YOUR CHURCH

nelson searcy

WITH JENNIFER DYKES HENSON

BakerBooks

a division of Baker Publishing Group
Grand Rapids, Michigan

Published by Baker Books
a division of Baker Publishing Group
PO Box 6287, Grand Rapids, MI 49516-6287
www.bakerbooks.com

Printed in the United States of America

Library of Congress Cataloging-in-Publication Data
Names: Searcy, Nelson, author. | Henson, Jennifer Dykes, author.
Title: Fusion : turning first-time guests into fully engaged members of your church / Nelson Searcy, with Jennifer Dykes Henson.
Description: Revised and expanded [edition]. | Grand Rapids : Baker Books, 2017. | Includes bibliographical references and index.
Identifiers: LCCN 2017026063 | ISBN 9780801075490 (pbk. : alk. paper)
Subjects: LCSH: Church membership.
Classification: LCC BV820 .S43 2017 | DDC 254/.5—dc23
LC record available at https://lccn.loc.gov/2017026063

19 20 21 22 23 24   8 7 6 5 4 3

contents

introduction
to the revised
and expanded edition

Everything you and I do as church leaders stems from one common goal: to lead people into a growing relationship with Jesus Christ. Our work is not about perfecting our worship sets and preaching, having the best intro videos in town, or bringing in crowds so that we can feel good about our numbers. None of these things are ends unto themselves, but only means to the end of introducing people to Jesus and helping them grow as his disciples. And that introduction begins the minute a first-time guest walks through our doors.

Since the original release of *Fusion: Turning First-Time Guests into Fully Engaged Members of Your Church*, the process for assimilating newcomers that is outlined in these pages has been tested, refined, improved, and proven time and time again not only by The Journey Church but also by the thousands of church leaders I have coached in the United

States and around the world. I stand on a track record of having trained well over three thousand churches to use the system that you are about to discover. Out of that number, there are literally thousands of success stories from church leaders who have implemented the Fusion system to revolutionize their growth and change lives.

In the pages ahead, you will have the opportunity to learn from those who have gone before you. This revised and expanded edition of *Fusion: Turning First-Time Guests into Fully Engaged Members of Your Church* is chock-full of new insights based on the cumulative positive experiences of the leaders who are using *Fusion* to keep the guests God sends from slipping through the cracks. You will discover well-tested and confirmed strategies for everything involved in helping guests walk the path from their first visit to their second visit to regular attendance and finally to membership, all the while introducing them to the love of Jesus and inviting them into a growing relationship with him.

When it comes to fusing newcomers into your congregation, small efforts reap big rewards. You don't have to be ready to implement the entire assimilation system presented here right away. Feel free to start small. By taking a few crucial steps—like developing a Connection Card culture (see chapter 4) or starting to send short, handwritten notes to your first-time guests (see chapter 5)—you can radically impact the number of first-timers who return again and again. Study the powerful system detailed ahead with an open heart and open mind. Then start implementing it at your own speed. God will honor your willingness to make the small changes in your church that can help shine his love to those first-time *gifts* he's graciously sending your way.

Partnering with God to connect people to his church is significant work. My prayer is that as you dive into the pages ahead—whether you have used the Fusion system before and are back for a refresher, whether you are a seasoned pastor looking for a way to reenergize your growth or are just beginning your journey of leading a church that reaches people for the kingdom—God will speak to your heart and mind as you prepare for the awe-inspiring task he has set before you.

foreword

I have given my GPS a name. I call her Linda. I don't know how I managed before Linda came into my life. She has been extremely helpful in strange cities and new situations. She has saved me time, given me confidence in my travels, and in some cases made the difference in whether or not I arrived at my destination at all.

The systems and insights you will find in the following pages could be your new GPS for assimilation. In this book, Nelson and Jennifer have done the hard work of naming the streets, identifying the landmarks, and highlighting the milestones so that the local church can help each individual with whom they come in contact to move from a mere guest to a fully engaged member who is serving and sharing Christ with others.

I met Nelson Searcy shortly after I made my first trip to New York City. I was deeply disturbed by the fact that there were so few churches making a difference in a city that could make such a difference in the world. On a human level, I knew that a church start in New York City would have its best chance if several key elements were in place: a critical mass in its launch team, adequate funding, a good location, and most of all, a leader with God-given strategic leadership abilities and communications skills. Somehow Nelson, who was thinking about starting a church in New York, heard through the ecclesiastical grapevine about the interest Lake Pointe (the church I pastor in Rockwall, Texas) had in New York City. He called, and what was supposed to be a short twenty-minute stop-by because Nelson was "going to be in town" turned into a four-hour lunch and subsequent partnership that helped produce a prevailing church in New York City.

You will be glad you picked up this book for the same reason I am glad we partnered with Nelson when we did— it's also the reason I personally look forward to our regular conversations. Nelson is more than a theorist. He is a practitioner—one who has hammered out an effective system of assimilation in a city where people resist assimilation like cats resist obedience training. But Nelson is also more than a practitioner. I have known guys who could hit the ball out of the park but could never tell anyone how to do the same. Nelson has the ability to capture essential transferable concepts and pass along that vital information to others.

Since the beginning of The Journey Church, Nelson has played the dual role of both player and coach. He has been quarterback for his own team while playing the role of coach for hundreds of church starts and existing churches all over the nation and now the world. He is a voracious reader and a maniacal social networker. These two traits give him a vast reservoir to draw from, as is evident in the creative, fresh, and strategic ways he approaches the challenges of local church ministry—one of which is assimilation.

Anyone who has ever attempted to lead a local church knows the importance of assimilation. I think it is ironic that Nelson has named the church he started in New York City "The Journey" because becoming assimilated in a community of faith is also a journey where one must move along a path that has a definite starting point, important milestones, and a destination. This book helps us as leaders by providing a clear map that we can share with others who are seeking to become all that God has called them to be. Very few people will be able to successfully complete their journey without both a clear map and someone to guide them.

Along with Nelson and Jennifer, I realize that assimilation is not the same thing as spiritual formation. Assimilation is integration into the local church as one moves from being merely a guest to becoming a fully engaged, responsible member of the local body of Christ. Spiritual formation is nothing less than being shaped into the image of Jesus Christ by the power of the Holy Spirit for the glory of God. However, we believe that God wants to use assimilation into and through the local church as a vital part of spiritual formation. Spiritual formation happens best in community where fellow believers encourage, confront, and then support one another in following Christ.

The metaphor of sailing is helpful at this point in our understanding. No matter how one sets the sails, the boat will go nowhere unless the wind blows. It is also true that even when the wind is blowing, if the sails are not correctly set and the boat is not positioned in a cooperative way, it still will not reach its destination. Assimilation is the process by which the local church helps individuals in the setting of their sails. But make no mistake about it—unless God is involved and his Spirit is blowing across our lives, no amount of structure in the church will produce spiritual growth.

My prayer is that *Fusion* will help you become clear about how to help others in your church set their sails so that when the wind of God blows, they can reach the destination that he desires.

Steve Stroope
Senior Pastor
Lake Pointe Church
Rockwall, Texas

preface

Turning first-time guests into fully engaged church members is a weighty spiritual responsibility. Every church and every church leader has an important role to play in making sure that no one God has called through the doors of a church slips through the cracks—which is why this book, and the system it contains within its pages, is so needed. *Fusion: Turning First-Time Guests into Fully Engaged Members of Your Church* is a critical read for the following people:

- executive and lead pastors
- pastors and staff who are responsible for connections, hospitality, or newcomer ministry
- all church staff interested in assimilating newcomers (which should be all staff members!)
- elders, deacons, or committee/team leaders
- volunteer teams working within newcomer ministry
- church leaders with a desire to experience healthy church growth

- church planters who are in prelaunch or the early stages of growth
- leaders of long-established churches struggling with stagnation
- denominational leaders who are involved in equipping churches
- seminary students who wish to study assimilation or church growth
- laypeople with a heart for supporting the ministry of their church
- students of church growth, church health, or church systems
- anyone looking for fresh ideas on how to help newcomers become fully developing followers of Jesus

For maximum impact, I suggest using this book as a tool for group study with other pastors, church leaders, and/or volunteer teams. Many additional support materials are available at www.FusionBook.com.

Thank you for preparing for the high calling God has given you to lead new people down the path toward spiritual maturity.

acknowledgments

Nelson:

First and foremost I would like to thank Jesus Christ for calling me to himself and his church.

I also want to thank all the committed Christians who had a part in helping me go from first-time guest to fully developing follower (although I'm still working on the "fully" part).

A sincere thank-you to my wife, Kelley, for her love, encouragement, and partnership in this and all the other projects God has allowed us to be a part of. I can't imagine doing the journey of life without her by my side.

I also want to express appreciation to my son, Alexander, who didn't have a choice in going to church as a first-time guest (his mom and I pushed him in a stroller to church without regard to his will or desires). As time proceeds, may he choose to follow God fully and freely.

Thanks also to Jennifer Henson, who (miraculously) turned my scribbles, audio seminars, transcripts, seminar notes, phone conversations, and emails into the book you now hold, and who uses her writing and communication skills to serve God and his church.

My thanks to Kerrick Thomas, who codeveloped the live seminar on which this book is based and who models the passion for God and people found in this book.

Finally, to the committed editors, publicists, and friends at Baker Books, I express deep gratitude. Books really do change the world.

Jennifer:

An ancient proverb teaches that wise parents give their children roots and wings. I am thankful to have been blessed with wise parents: my father, who taught me to fly, and my mother, who knew I was a writer long before I did and always kept me on course.

Thanks to my husband, Brian, for filling every day of the journey with laughter and love. And to my two incredible daughters, Isabelle and Ivey-Grace, for brightening my world in immeasurable ways.

Thanks also to Nelson, for consistently remaining true to the vision God has given him and for inviting me into it over a decade ago. Every year and every book is better than the last.

introduction

Insanity is doing the same thing over and over
again and expecting different results.

Albert Einstein

I will build my church, and all the powers of hell
will not conquer it.

Jesus (Matt. 16:18)

Next Sunday the Spirit of God will prompt hundreds of
thousands of people in the United States and millions around
the world to visit a church for the first time. The Sunday
after that, he will do it again. God is constantly blessing his
church with regular guests. The question is: *Are you and I
doing all we can to accept and honor his blessing?*

The first congregation I pastored met in a small wooden
church building on the outskirts of Charlotte, North Carolina. Thanks to the church's position on top of a hill, the

steeple could be seen clearly from the closest major road. The gravel parking lot was a little outdated, but it underscored the place's simple ambiance. After I had been there for about a year, God had grown our congregation to record attendance: fifty people a week.

During that time, I began to notice something extraordinary. We were averaging one or two first-time guests each Sunday. Over the course of a few months, I determined that our average number of guests per week was 1.5. This meant that over the course of a year, we had between seventy-five and eighty first-time guests coming through our doors. Astonishing! I was struck by the realization that our little congregation could more than double in a year if we were able to keep every first-time guest God was sending us. The need for and power of assimilation began sinking into my psyche.

Fast-forward almost a decade. My wife, Kelley, and I had just moved to New York City to pursue the vision God had given us to grow a church from scratch. When we arrived in the steamy heat of a city summer, we had no money, no members, and no meeting location. But, as he often does, God worked in miraculous ways and we officially launched The Journey Church of the City the following Easter, with 110 people in attendance. (For a detailed guide on starting a healthy church, see my book *Launch: Starting a New Church from Scratch*.)

We were ecstatic that God had sent that many people to us—but the excitement didn't last long. The next week, I learned my first church growth principle: everyone who attends church on Easter doesn't come back the following Sunday. Fifty-five of our 110 attendees returned. Not too bad, we thought; we had kept half. Yet over the next five months, with my dynamic leadership and powerful preaching, I grew the church down to thirty-five, in a city of eight million.

I was discouraged. One Sunday, on my way home after a service with our small crowd, I humbled myself before God. I remember praying something like this:

God, I know you've called me to New York City and you've made it possible for me to start this church. I'll stay here for the rest of my life and pastor a church of thirty-five if that's what you want. But God, I have to believe that there is more. I believe you want me to tell as many people as possible in this city about Jesus. And right now things seem to be going in the wrong direction. If this keeps up, we'll be back down to just Kelley and me by Christmas!

Over the next several weeks, God began to open my eyes to many things about our new church. Two revelations, in particular, apply directly to this discussion in these pages. First, God reminded me that my church was not really my church. It was his church. His heart for the people of New York was much larger than mine. God showed me that my responsibility was to follow his lead as he used me to grow the church his way—not to try to initiate growth on my own. Of course, I knew this when I set out to begin The Journey, but as I faced the daily rigors of starting a church, I had let it fall to the back of my mind. Once again, I affirmed that I would follow after God as he built his church. (See Matt. 16:18.)

Second, God prompted me to do some research on our church's brief history. I sensed him leading me to go back and look at the Sunday attendance numbers for the last five months. At this point, we weren't as systematic about tracking weekly vital signs as we are now, but I did have a record of attendance, offering numbers, and the estimated number of first-time guests. (We were still small enough for me to eyeball the newcomers.) I added up the total number of first-time guests God had sent our way over the previous five months and was, again, stunned. We were averaging between three and four first-time adult guests every week. Over that twenty-week period of decline from April to August, we'd had close to eighty first-time guests—eighty gifts from God that I had failed to accept graciously. The number jumped off the page at me. I found myself humbled before God yet again, praying:

God, you've entrusted us with almost eighty guests over the last few weeks. I'm sorry for how little we've done to prepare for their coming or to follow up with them after their visit. I believe these are unchurched people you have given to our care, and I've been a poor shepherd.

After that period of acknowledgment and repentance, we began to take a hard look at everything related to first-time guests, from their initial experience to follow-up. Beginning that fall through the following spring, God worked through us and developed, by way of its very implementation, what has become known as the "Fusion assimilation system." We packaged this system as a live training event, with a workbook and audio resource. To our surprise, during the next twenty-four months, 3,500 churches used all or part of our system—with incredible results!

Over the last several years, the system you'll find detailed in the pages ahead has turned into nothing short of an assimilation movement. I have had the opportunity to train thousands of pastors both in the United States and around the world, helping them to implement a proven strategy for assimilating the gifts God sends to his churches each and every week. Through one-on-one personal coaching and through large assimilation training events, my team and I have helped dedicated church leaders discover how to lead newcomers down the path from being first-time guests to being growing, committed, fully engaged Jesus followers and church members. (For more on my personal coaching and training events, go to www.FusionBook.com.)

Oh, what happened at The Journey after my moment of realization and that humbling conversation with God? Well, from the low point of 35, we grew back to a weekly average attendance of 110 over the next four months. The following year, we broke 300 for the first time, and 500 the year after that. Over the next two years, we began averaging 1,000 people in attendance each week, including an average of 35 first-time guests. During those four instrumental years, we saw over 600 people come to faith in Christ for the first time.

Since then, The Journey Church has grown to include multiple locations in Manhattan and the outer boroughs, plus a location in Boca Raton, Florida. All of our locations' average attendance and first-time guest numbers we could only have dreamed of during that first rocky year. Many things have changed during our years of growth, but one important thing has remained consistent: we are determined to connect with and fully assimilate every first-time guest God sends our way.

I have been praying for you as this book has made its way into your hands. Time and time again, I have seen God dramatically change the culture and direction of a church when concerned leaders decided to focus on how they handle first-time guests. As we begin our journey together, I challenge you to listen to God, honestly examine your process for taking people from being first-time guests to members, and honestly address changes that may need to be made as you move toward more effective assimilation. Let's get started!

1

the power of assimilation

It is not enough to do your best; you must know what to do, and then do your best.

W. Edwards Deming

Well done, good and faithful servant! You have been faithful with a few things. I will put you in charge of many things.

Jesus (Matt. 25:21 NIV)

How do you feel about thank-you cards? Are you one of those people who sends them for everything? For Christmas gifts and casual lunches? Or do you reserve the gesture for truly special or unexpected courtesies? My wife, Kelley, and I come down on different sides of this issue. She grew up in a family where thank-you cards were a way of life. She couldn't wait to get started on them after our honeymoon. When baby shower time came, she was on a thank-you card mission. Of course, I was completely on board with getting these done quickly, but the idea of sending thank-you cards for birthday gifts was a little foreign to me. While I still say there's a fine line between graciousness and overkill, I have come to understand that receiving a gift always demands some form of reciprocity. I've also begun to realize that my response—or lack of response—to a gift speaks volumes to the giver.

During my years of ministry, I have messed this up more times than I care to admit. My slips have taught me that failing to say thank you to the right people at the right time leads to embarrassment. I'm sure you know what I mean. Has anyone ever given you a gift and you just never got around to saying a proper thank-you? After a few weeks or months, didn't it hit the point where you were embarrassed to acknowledge your innocent inaction and found yourself avoiding that person—and an uncomfortable situation—altogether?

Not long ago, a couple in our church gave me a great, unexpected gift. They were not members and hadn't been around very long. I wasn't sure of their last name or where they lived, and the card they included with the gift didn't help me out at all. Without their last name, I couldn't track down an address to thank them properly. At first, I found myself looking out for them on Sundays so I could thank them personally, but I never seemed to catch them. The more time that passed, the more embarrassed I got. After about a month, I began hoping I wouldn't run into them and wondering what they thought of my apparent rudeness. We've all been there, right?

Here's another truth I've discovered: what you do with a gift you've been given speaks volumes about your level of appreciation. You may say thank you to the giver or even send a nice note, but what happens to the gift itself? Do you toss it, still in the box, to the corner of your room where it collects dust until it becomes useless? Or do you examine it thoughtfully, cut off the tags, and integrate it into your life? Actions always speak louder than words. How you respond when you've been given a gift—and what you do with the gift itself—proves just how much you really appreciate it.

So, have you been given any gifts lately?

Let me ask the question another way: Did you have any first-time guests at your church last week? How many guests have you had in the last month? Over the last year? Each of those guests was a gift from God to you. How did you receive them? Did your response show the Giver your appreciation? Did you handle those gifts in the way they deserved by having a plan in place to integrate them into the life of your church? Or did you just say a quick thank-you and move on? Maybe you would have liked to do more to show your thanks, but you weren't sure of the best approach. Like me with my mystery givers, you may have wanted to respond with more excitement, but you didn't know how.

Assimilation leads to life transformation by giving people the means and opportunity to become maturing followers of Christ.

God gives you and me the gifts we call first-time guests freely—and strategically. He expects us to handle what we've been given with similar strategic care. First-time guests are full of unparalleled potential. As God brings them through our front doors, our prayerfully planned reciprocation can result in changed lives for the kingdom. God has set up the perfect win-win scenario. He is bringing us the new faces. Our responsibility is to show our gratitude and commitment by doing our part to turn those new faces into new fully developing members.

Why Assimilate?

Assimilation leads to life transformation by giving people the means and opportunity to become maturing followers of Christ. In broad terms, assimilation can be defined as the process used to encourage your first-time guests to continue coming back until they see and understand God's power, accept Jesus as their Savior, and commit themselves to the local church through membership.

As you think about the power of assimilation, consider Paul's example. Paul's heart cry for the Galatians was that Christ would be fully formed in their lives. Everything he did for them and all of his exhortation was with that one purpose in mind. He wanted them to be unhindered in their quest to know Jesus and follow him closely.

Do you have the same passion for your church? For your community? Isn't that why you went into ministry in the first place? When God called you to serve him, did he call you to maintain the status quo, or did he call you to see that Christ would be truly revealed and reflected through the lives of those he would entrust to your care?

At The Journey, the crux of assimilation is also the heart of our overall mission: to give people the best possible opportunity to become fully developing followers of Jesus

Christ. We know, as I'm sure you do, that the majority of people who visit a church do not come to faith in Christ on their first visit—or their second or third. Instead, continued interaction with God's people, teaching from the Bible, and involvement in volunteer opportunities all work together to open unchurched hearts to the good news of Jesus Christ.

Encouraging people to stick around our churches is not about making our auditoriums look full and our numbers impressive; it's about leading them to faith in Jesus, through the Spirit's prompting. Putting a strong, strategic assimilation system in place is the best way to ensure that our newcomers will stay with us long enough to respond to Christ's pull. (To see an outline of The Journey's assimilation process, turn to appendix A. For a downloadable version, visit www .FusionBook.com.)

A Numbers Game

I'm sure you know how the critics think: To those of us who advocate healthy, growing churches, it's all about the numbers, right? Well, the critics are right to an extent: we do care about numbers. Why? Because every number represents a life. In a properly facilitated assimilation system, the number of new members you have is a reflection of the number of new lives in your church that belong to Christ. Your regular attenders represent people in the process of becoming fully developing followers of Jesus. Your guest count gauges the effectiveness of your evangelism and outreach. When grounded in the right perspective, numbers are an indication of life change. They are a testimony that

God is at work. But anyone who looks at numbers with a competitive spirit or who wants to grow a church for growth's sake alone, without life change being the driving force, is not truly in alignment with the heart of the Great Commission.

Not one person who comes through your doors comes haphazardly. By sending a guest to you, God is giving you the privilege of cooperating with him to move someone forward in his or her journey toward Jesus. When you have a clear plan in place to make your guest feel welcome, to encourage the person to return as a second-time guest, to keep that individual coming as a regular attender, to see the person accept Jesus and to decide to commit to your church through membership, then do you get to include that person in your number count? Well, only as a by-product. More important, you get to rejoice over another person saying yes to God's will for his or her life. You get to glorify God with another person who came to you unchurched and now wants to commit to the local fellowship. It's never about numbers for numbers' sake—it's about the people the numbers represent.

Context: Crowd to Congregation

The Circles of Commitment were conceptualized by Rick Warren to define the progressive levels a person moves through as he or she becomes committed to the local church. In *The Purpose-Driven Church: Growth without Compromising Your Message and Mission*, Warren contends that the goal of a living, growing church is "to move people from the outer circle (low commitment/low spiritual maturity) to the inner circle (high commitment/high spiritual maturity)."[1]

The assimilation system detailed in the following pages builds the bridge for people to cross from the realm of the "crowd" into the realm of the "congregation." I fully believe that when new people visit your church and establish themselves as part of the crowd, you are embarking on a journey with those people. If you commit to guiding them across the bridge of assimilation, you are giving them the best opportunity to respond to God and give their lives to Jesus. Once they sincerely profess faith, they will have fulfilled the number one requirement for taking the official step of membership and moving into the congregation. But before that bridge can be crossed, it has to be built.

Ratio Reality

To get started, ask yourself: *How well am I assimilating people now?* It's time to check your church's vital signs. In order to find your assimilation ratio, which is the measure of your current assimilation rate, you need to know:

31

(1) how many regular attenders you have,

(2) how many guests you have, and

(3) how many of those guests stay.

Understanding how the numbers work within your church is critical to monitoring the success of your assimilation system. Let's step inside Fictional Community Church (FCC) for a moment and see how well they are assimilating first-time guests.

Tim is the pastor of FCC, a church with a regular attendance of 430. Tim estimates that FCC averages about ten first-time guests each week. He knows that a healthy ratio of first-timers to regular attenders is 5/100, or five guests for every one hundred regulars.

FCC's ratio is about 2.5/100, which puts him just below maintenance mode. Three first-time guests for every one hundred attenders is the minimum number of guests that FCC, or any church, needs just to maintain consistency as people move away, join other churches, or die. Five guests per one hundred regular attenders usually signals a growing church, while seven guests per one hundred regular attenders would indicate rapid growth. Even though Tim is not seeing as many first-time guests as he would like or even as many as he saw a couple of years ago, the real

---

Ratio of First-Time Guests to Regular Attenders

3/100 = a church in maintenance mode
5/100 = a steadily growing church
7/100 = a rapidly growing church

---

question weighing on Tim is: *What is happening to those who do visit?*

If Tim has had an average of ten guests each week over the course of a fifty-week year (for the sake of simple math, we'll give him two Sundays off), that means he has had five hundred first-time guests come through his doors in the last twelve months. But looking back over the year's growth numbers, Tim realizes that FCC has only grown by sixty people in the same period of time. Huh?

Tim gets down to business and decides to figure out his actual assimilation ratio. If FCC had five hundred guests attend over the last year and ultimately kept sixty of those guests as new members, FCC has an assimilation ratio of roughly 1/8—one out of every eight guests becomes integrated with the church. Tim wonders about the other seven guests in that equation, or the other 440 people. What happened to them? How did they slip through? Just think: if Tim were able to get his assimilation ratio up to one out of five people returning, he could grow by an additional forty people over the next year. That would be a total of one hundred new members!

With the numbers in front of him, Tim decides to make some changes. He's not planning to revamp other areas of FCC—just to focus more intently on the kind of experience his first-time guests are having and to start taking a harder look at how they walk the path from their first visit to membership. By taking small steps to ensure that guests want to return, he will dramatically increase the number of people who stay connected with the church long enough to understand God's will for their lives.

Over the next several months, Tim reevaluates and restructures his assimilation system. The results are almost immediate. As Tim honors God by valuing guests who come through his door, God honors Tim by showing himself at FCC in a mighty way.

How do the assimilation numbers look for your church? When you get right down to it, how are you doing at keeping the guests God gives you?

Those of you who are researchers and number crunchers are going to love the rest of this chapter. I am going to ask you to do a little digging into your own assimilation ratio.

Where Am I?

In order to really go to work on your assimilation rate, you first need to figure out where you are—your assimilation ratio. Do this by following the steps below. For maximum benefit, I suggest that you do the research on your church as you continue reading. Don't let this process cause you to stall. If you are reading this as a team, perhaps you could divide up the tasks of looking back over your records and finding the numbers you need.

1. Determine your average attendance two years ago, or as far back as you can since then. I suggest pulling your attendance numbers from March or October, as those are generally good growth months.

   Average attendance number in

   _____ = _____

   Month/Two Years Ago

2. Determine your average attendance for the same month one year ago.

   Average attendance number in

   _____ = _____

   Month/One Year Ago

3. Subtract the two-year-old attendance number from the one-year-old attendance number. The difference is your net growth.

   Net growth = _____

4. Determine the total number of first-time guests you had during that period of time. You can figure this number by adding up the actual number of first-timers you had (if you have that information) or by estimating how many guests you averaged each week and multiplying by 52.

   Total number of first-timers during same period = _____

5. Divide your net growth by your total number of first-time guests.

   Net growth/Total number of first-timers = _____

6. Divide 1 by that number to get your second ratio number. Round it to the nearest digit.

   My assimilation ratio = 1/_____

The number you just discovered is your assimilation ratio, or as it is sometimes called, your assimilation rate. It represents the number of first-time guests you are keeping. The examples below will help illuminate and clarify what the assimilation ratio looks like for different types of churches.

Example 1—Minimal Growth

Average attendance October of last year	305.0
Average attendance October of this year	307.0
Net gain	2.0
First-time guests between last October and this October	156.0
Net gain/Number of first-timers	0.013
1/.013 = 77, which equals an assimilation ratio of 1/77	

Note: This doesn't mean that this church didn't reach new people. The church may have reached a lot of new people and may have also lost many long-term members. An array of factors could have contributed to the small net gain. If you've ever pastored a church, you know there are times when any net gain is a miracle.

Example 2—Steady Growth

Average attendance October of last year	210.0
Average attendance October of this year	255.0
Net gain	45.0
First-time guests between last October and this October	208.0
Net gain/Number of first-timers	0.216
1/.21 = 4.6, which rounds to an assimilation rate of 1/5	

Example 3—Fast Growth

Average attendance October of last year	110.0
Average attendance October of this year	327.0
Net gain	217.0
First-time guests between last October and this October	364.0
Net gain/Number of first-timers	0.596
1/.596 = 1.67, which rounds to an assimilation rate of 1/2	

Note: This fast-growing church is keeping about three people for every five guests. I have seen this exact scenario play out many times in new churches or churches that experience dramatic turnaround. For more on this, see my book *Launch: Starting a New Church from Scratch*.

Example 4—The Very Large Church	
Average attendance October of last year	2,200.0
Average attendance October of this year	2,800.0
Net gain	600.0
First-time guests between last October and this October	9,400.0
Net gain/Number of first-timers	0.063
1/.063 = 16, which equals an assimilation rate of 1/16	

Note: You can see that size doesn't necessarily mean a better assimilation rate. But size does mean that a few changes in assimilation can reap big rewards. For example, if this church had seen a mere 1/10 assimilation rate during the same period, they would have grown by 940 people instead of 600. That's an additional 340 people by doing nothing but changing their assimilation process.

In training thousands of churches on the Fusion assimilation system, I've found that the average leader I work with is experiencing about a 1/20 assimilation rate. That rate translates to some growth. While anything better than 1/20 should lead to solid growth, I suggest that you pray for an assimilation rate of 1/3.

Be careful not to fool yourself if you feel like your assimilation rate is already better than most—just because you have a strong rate doesn't mean you are doing all you can do. Your rate can always get better. At the same time, a low rate doesn't mean there's no hope. God wants those first-timers he sends you to be assimilated. You just need to make the commitment to be honest about where you are right now and where you are going.

Where Am I Going?

Now that you know your assimilation ratio, it's time to think about where you want to go. The pages ahead will show you the heart and mechanics behind creating a system of assimilation that will revolutionize your church.

Decide not to let any of the gifts God sends you go unreciprocated. Show him your gratitude by treating your newcomers with the grace, understanding, and hospitality that are reflective of his own character. By putting a well-planned, well-executed assimilation system into place, you will be doing your part to ensure that the first-time guests who cross your path are transformed into fully developing followers of Jesus. If you take to heart the concepts presented here, you soon will be able to look back and say with Paul:

> This is good and pleases God our Savior, who wants everyone to be saved and to understand the truth. (1 Tim. 2:3–4)

2

biblical hospitality

> If you can't describe what you are doing as a process, you don't know what you're doing.
>
> W. Edwards Deming

> For even the Son of Man came not to be served but to serve others.
>
> Jesus (Mark 10:45)

As the old saying goes: *If you fail to plan, you plan to fail.* This is particularly true for preparatory planning and could just as pointedly be stated: *If you fail to prepare, you prepare to fail.* Preparation is key to success in any endeavor.

To leave your house in the morning, you have to prepare yourself. You shower, comb your hair, and brush your teeth, right? If you don't, you won't be ready to face the world.

If you have a meeting to attend or a presentation to give, you study, review, and practice what you are going to say. To cook a meal, you find the recipe, make sure you have all the ingredients, and pull out the pots and pans you'll need.

Likewise, when it comes to running your church, you prepare. Every week you get ready for the service: You plan the preaching, the music, and the special speakers. You plan the children's activities. You work tirelessly until you are prepared for every aspect of the weekend—but are you ready for the guests who will be joining you? It has been said that, "The church is a family expecting guests." Is your family ready?

Imagine I've invited you into my home for dinner. I would put a lot of effort into getting ready for your visit. I would take the piled-up newspapers out to the recycling bin, pick up the toys in the hallway, and even run a dust rag over the furniture. I would want to make sure that my home gave the best possible impression of me. When you arrive, I would show you around, make sure you know where the bathroom is, and give you a comfortable place to sit. For our meal, I would make something I know you would enjoy. In short, I would do everything in my power to make you feel welcome and respected as a guest in my home. By preparing in advance for your coming, I would be able to treat you with the hospitality you deserve.

The church—your church—truly is a family expecting guests. And you should be ready to show them intentional hospitality when they arrive. While they are in your company, they need to feel comfortable and valued, no matter where they are in their spiritual development. When they leave, be proactive in giving them a return invitation they'll be hard-pressed to refuse. Your church is a representation of the bigger family of God. As you put a system in place to effectively integrate guests into the family, you will be fulfilling part of the responsibility God placed on you when he prompted them your way. God is honored when you show your guests true biblical hospitality.

Defining Service

If you've ever visited a Ritz-Carlton, you know that they live by the company motto: "We are ladies and gentlemen serving ladies and gentlemen." As an organization, they epitomize hospitable service. When I was in seminary in Durham, North Carolina, the Ritz-Carlton in Washington, DC, would periodically advertise special low one-night rates in our local newspaper. Occasionally, Kelley and I would take advantage of the opportunity to get away, hop into our old, run-down car, and head north for a night in luxury.

The first time we visited the Ritz-Carlton, I was amazed. As soon as I pulled into their circular driveway, a bellman ran over, opened my door, and said to his colleague, "The gentleman from North Carolina has arrived!"

I didn't know what to concentrate on first—the fact that he had been astute enough to notice my license plate or the fact that he had just called me a gentleman. That was new! Then he rushed to the other side of the car and politely escorted Kelley out of her seat as he asked me, "Whom are we welcoming to the Ritz-Carlton?"

After glancing over my shoulder to make sure he was still talking to me, I stuttered my name. Again, the bellman immediately relayed the information to his partner, "Mr. and Mrs. Searcy have arrived." He then ushered us inside to check in.

Later that evening, we happened to run into the same bellman while on our way to dinner. Without hesitation, he looked me in the eye and said, "Have a good night, Mr. Searcy." Impressive.

Such stellar guest interaction does not happen by default. Ritz-Carlton employees are trained on the importance of creating a welcoming atmosphere for every person who chooses to walk through their doors. They are taught to greet you, know your name by the second time they see you, and not let you leave without a sincere thank-you and good-bye. With a strong system in place to clear the path toward effectiveness, the Ritz-Carlton is able to consistently treat their guests well. The staff is empowered to represent their organization with the intrinsic pride it deserves, and they see the results in an unusually high repeat-guest rate.

You may be thinking: *So? The Ritz-Carlton is a hotel. A business. That's what they are supposed to do. What does that have to do with the church?* More than most of us like to acknowledge. Unfortunately, the business world often understands more about true hospitality than the church does. As Jesus taught, "It is true that the children of this world are more shrewd in dealing with the world around them than are the children of the light" (Luke 16:8).

Just step back and take a look. While hotels, restaurants, and stores all around us serve their guests with intentional care, we often let ours wander in and out of our weekly services with no specific plan for showing them how important they are to us.

The Ritz-Carlton is in the business of sleep. Their single goal is to make you feel good about spending your money with them so that you will do it again, simply for a nice place to lay your head. We, on the other hand, are in the business of eternity. We are in God's business. Yet we focus less time and energy on engaging our guests than the people who provide theirs with little more than a comfortable bed and a hot shower.

The new people who walk through our doors have the opportunity to come into relationship with their Creator, a chance to discover his will for their lives, and the ability to step into their place in his family—and we take our part in that opportunity for granted. We have not taught our staff or our congregations to serve guests with grace and hospitality. We have not internalized the gravity of our burden to reflect God's character in the way we treat them. We do not have a plan in place to encourage their continual return. We are not prepared.

Understanding the importance of assimilation may require you to change the way you think about service. God has not only given us the responsibility of being hospitable to his guests, but he has also given us the perfect example of how to go about it. Jesus came to the earth to serve, not to be served. Throughout the New Testament, we see his examples of selfless service for those he had the opportunity to influence. And we've been left with the challenge of doing even greater things. That is a high challenge, especially when it comes to caring for those who may not yet know him. When we serve our guests well, we reflect Jesus's attitude and mind-set toward them.

When we serve our guests well, we reflect Jesus's attitude and mind-set. toward them.

Assimilation is simply well-planned biblical hospitality. The head of our organization is the greatest server of all time. Doesn't it follow that we should be the ultimate example of service to our guests? With the right system in place, we can serve in a way that will truly touch lives for God's kingdom.

The Assimilation System

A well-developed assimilation system will give you a strategic process for integrating newcomers into your church, with the goal of helping them become fully developing followers of Christ. As I have mentioned, the system presented here has worked well at The Journey and in other churches across the country and around the world. Still, I invite you to take the overarching principles to heart and customize the details to fit your church's environment. The specifics that work for city-dwelling twenty- and thirtysomethings may not impact suburban forty- and fiftysomethings quite the same way. So work with the system. Internalize its lessons and themes. Learn from the examples that follow, and then make it your own. God has breathed life and blessing into this system of welcoming people to the body. He is the source of its effectiveness. Trust the Spirit, and use the system.

The Fusion assimilation system is built around a three-step process that leads guests from their first visit to their participation in a Membership Class:

Step One—Turn a first-time guest into a second-time guest.

Step Two—Turn a second-time guest into a regular attender.

Step Three—Turn a regular attender into a fully developing member.

As your new people approach each of these steps, you must have short-term goals in place that will make the transitions clear and accessible. In other words, you must have a defined picture of how first-time guests bridge the gap to become second-time guests. Then you must fully understand the necessary thought process and actions needed for those people to take the next big step to regular attendance. And you must be able to articulate exactly what has to happen to help your regular attenders become ready to take the step of membership. Clarity at each turn is key.

Not only do you have to understand the specific goals of each step, but you also have to have a plan in place that will encourage every new person in your care to achieve these goals. Your newcomers don't know what they don't know, and they are looking to you for guidance—whether they realize it or not.

Bridging the Gaps

In the last chapter, we saw how the Fusion assimilation system builds a bridge allowing those in the crowd to cross into the congregation. That big bridge is composed of three sections—three smaller bridges, if you will—that allow your guests to move from Step One to Step Two to Step Three. Take a look at the diagram of The Journey's process below.

The white spaces, or gaps, along the arrow's path need to be bridged in order for your first-timers to step from one

JOURNEY ASSIMILATION PROCESS

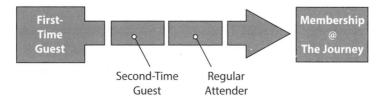

box to the next. You certainly don't want to lose anyone in those cracks. Churches that have a lot of first-time guests but few new members are losing their people in these gaps. They don't have a clear-cut process for moving their guests toward integration, so their wandering newcomers wander right off the edge. The Fusion assimilation system bridges these gaps, providing a smooth path for every new person to walk on a journey from first-time guest to member.

ASSIMILATION BUZZWORDS

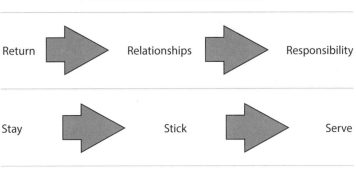

The pages that follow will give you the plans and tools you need to build your bridges. You will begin to see what really goes into a first-time guest's decision to *return* or *stay*. You will discover that *relationships* are the glue that encourages a second-time guest to *stick*. And you will have a chance to explore the way *responsibilities*, such as *serving*, lead to the sense of ownership that precedes membership. These buzzwords will become part of your team's lingo as you set up the process that will lead to their reality for each of your newcomers. Recite them often as you work to close the gaps on your guests' path to becoming fully developing followers of Christ.

The Power of Preparation

> Let us not become weary in doing good, for at the proper time we will reap a harvest if we do not give up. (Gal. 6:9 NIV)

In working with churches of all shapes and sizes, I have noticed an interesting phenomenon: the more prepared a church is to receive guests, the more guests it receives. Makes sense, doesn't it? Why would God send new people to a church that is not ready to welcome and nurture them? He will never give us more than we are prepared to handle. Scripture is filled with "If you . . . I will" scenarios. God wants us to show him, through our actions, that we can be trusted. If we prove faithful in preparing the way for the guests he has given us and for the guests we hope to receive, he will pour out his blessing by sending new people in our direction. Let's start preparing for the harvest.

3

seven minutes
and counting

We don't know where our first impressions come from or precisely what they mean, so we don't always appreciate their fragility.

Malcolm Gladwell

Be sure that everything is done properly and in order.

Apostle Paul (1 Cor. 14:40)

The human subconscious is a complex and powerful entity. While most of us float through life unaware of its influence, our subconscious is constantly shaping our thoughts, experiences, reactions, and opinions. As one researcher notes:

The mind operates most efficiently by relegating a good deal of high-level, sophisticated thinking to the unconscious, just as a modern jetliner is able to fly on automatic pilot with little or no input from the human, "conscious" pilot. The adaptive unconscious does an excellent job of sizing up the world . . . in a sophisticated and efficient manner.[1]

This God-given autopilot mechanism revs into action when we face unfamiliar territory, and tells us how to respond to our surroundings or our situation based on any number of outside clues. The feelings we get when we are introduced to new people or new places, whether positive or negative, are not the result of logical evaluation. They are based on instinct rather than reasoning.

More than likely, none of us are psychologists or neuro-geniuses, and we don't need to be. But if we want to successfully assimilate first-time guests into our congregations, we do need to at least recognize and embrace the power of the subconscious mind and the role that it plays in forming that all-important first impression.

The Power of a First Impression

Seven minutes is all you get to make a positive first impression. In the first seven minutes of contact with your church, your first-time guests will decide whether they are coming back. That's before a single worship song is sung and before a single word of the message is uttered.

Obviously your guests aren't making a logical decision based on the integrity of the preaching, the character of the church staff, or the clarity of your doctrine in these first seven minutes. They are not weighing pros and cons of worship styles and theological viewpoints. Instead, they are taking in clues about your church's atmosphere and people's friendliness on a much more rudimentary level. Their subconscious minds are working overtime to evaluate their compatibility with the new environment they've walked into.

This reality must prompt you and me to ask: *What's actually being judged? What factors and/or feelings play into their impression? And how much control do we have over doing things in a way that will make their experience ring positive?*

To get a glimpse of the power of your church's first impression on a guest, let's step to the other side and look at the experience from a guest's point of view.

It's Friday afternoon. Jon checks the clock on his desk, willing the hour hand to move faster. He can't wait for the weekend. He's got no real plans, except to throw some burgers on the grill and maybe catch the early baseball game on Sunday. He's about to jump online to see if he can get good seats when Sam knocks on his door. Oh, no. Sam has been trying to get him to visit his church for a couple of months now, and Jon's starting to run out of excuses. Before Jon knows what's happened, Sam has talked him into promising away his Sunday morning.

Sunday morning. Jon hits the blaring alarm clock and nudges Liz to get up. Even though she has been talking for years about going back to church, Liz was less than thrilled with the idea of following through this weekend. She had already planned a playdate for the kids. But Jon assured her that giving over one morning to FCC (Fictional

Community Church) would be well worth getting Sam off of his back.

Reluctantly Jon and Liz get up, and their morning plays out like something from a Stephen King novel. The kids, four and two, both throw temper tantrums, the eggs burn, and the dog smuggles his latest catch into the house. Tired, irritated, and already running late, Jon finally gets everyone packed into the car, and off they go.

Let's pause for a reality check. When an unchurched person or family decides to attend your church for the first time, what do you think is going to happen to them the morning of the service? The enemy is going to throw every obstacle he can in their direction. If he can't keep them from attending, he will at least make sure they hit the parking lot stressed and in no mood for what lies ahead. The enemy knows that if he can sow pre-service defensiveness and negativity, eight out of ten churches won't do anything to turn those guests' attitude around. In fact, in most cases, the church will just make the newcomers self-conscious, uncomfortable, and, by default, more irritable. Sadly, by nudging guests to disengage before they walk through the door, the devil usually wins the battle before it begins. But he can't win if we refuse to let him keep the upper hand—and that's where the Fusion assimilation system officially kicks in.

The Pre-service: From the Street to the Seat

The pre-service is your first opportunity for interaction with everyone who sets foot on your church's property—from guests to members—but its purpose and influence are particularly important for first-time guests. Your pre-service mission is to take your guests' guard down and even put a smile on their faces—before the service begins. Always assume that they've had a rough morning and have decided to make it to church anyway, and then do everything you can to make them feel welcome and glad they made it.

There are four initial areas of contact through which you can influence your guests during the pre-service—through controlling how they are *greeted*, *directed*, *treated*, and *seated*. Take a look at how a successful FCC pre-service would play out, and then we'll break down the details of each of the four pre-service components.

Jon and his family drive into the parking lot of the church and are immediately impressed by what they see. The building, though not large or even new, is obviously well cared for, right down to the lawn. Everyone is entering through the main front door, where a nice-looking couple about Jon and Liz's age is speaking warmly to each person and handing him or her some kind of program. (You might call it a bulletin, but since Jon and Liz are unchurched, they are more likely to think of it as a program.)

Once through the front door themselves, where they are welcomed with a smile and a "Glad you are here," Liz immediately spots two signs telling her exactly what she needs to know: one points the way to the restroom that her four-year-old urgently needs, and the other points toward the childcare area. After stop number one, Jon, Liz, and the kids check the childcare sign again and start in the direction it's pointing. A volunteer spots them and offers to lead them directly to the right place for each of their children.

When the kids have been dropped off, Jon notices the smell of coffee and donuts wafting toward him. He turns to discover a table piled with Krispy Kreme boxes, fruit, and coffee. He and Liz exchange pleasantly surprised glances, and then each grab a donut (well, she grabs an apple and he grabs a donut) and a cup of coffee and start timidly toward one of the aisles. Immediately, another volunteer steps up and directs them to two open seats. Jon begins to realize that the foul mood he drove into the parking lot with has been brightened a little by the smiles around him, the warm coffee in his hand, and the overall atmosphere of FCC. The people seem friendly and actually happy that he and Liz are there. At the church they used to go to, people hardly offered a smile, much less helpful information or Krispy Kremes—and he's always thought all churches were the same. As the service begins, Jon spots Sam just sitting down a few rows away. He can't help but wonder what's going on in this place.

Creating an environment that makes your first-time guests feel welcomed and respected is key to a successful assimilation system. When God entrusts you with first-time guests, you face an incredible responsibility. Those newcomers will likely make a decision about their return visit before they make it to their seats, based on the subconscious and conscious tools of evaluation God has blessed them with. You can acknowledge your guests as the gifts that they are by having a pre-service system in place that will far exceed their expectations and create that elusive positive first impression. You'll excite them to want to visit your church again and again so that they can ultimately learn about the excellence, graciousness, hospitality, and generosity of the One after whom you are modeling the system of their assimilation.

Now that we've seen Jon and Liz's successful pre-service experience, let's dive more deeply into each of its four components.

1. Greeted

Memorize the next sentence and embed it into your thinking: *Everything speaks to first-time guests—everything.* From the moment guests set foot on your property, they tune in to receive the message your church is sending. And your church is always sending a message, whether you realize it or not. The condition of your building, your sign, your grass, and your parking lot all speak to guests. Gut-level judgment calls are already being made. This does not necessarily mean the people are being overly critical (although this may be the case, depending on their history with the church) but just being human. They are reading their environment.

Knowing this, you have to make sure you are sending a welcoming message. You have an obligation to strive for excellence. You don't have to be perfect; you just have to do

---

The Four Components of the Pre-service

1. *Greeted:* Welcomed with a smile
2. *Directed:* Simply and politely shown to where they need to go
3. *Treated:* Happily surprised with comfort food/drink
4. *Seated:* Led to comfortable, appropriate seats

---

the best you can with what you've got, which is our definition of excellence.

You don't have to have a brand-new building or a big shiny sign to make a good impression, but chipped paint and overgrown grass will certainly make a bad one. Too often we are so familiar with the way our buildings and land look that we stop seeing them. So take a fresh look around. Drive into your parking lot and intentionally examine your church through a guest's eyes. Are you communicating the right message?

New York City is a renter's culture, even when it comes to church facilities. The Journey doesn't own a location. Instead, we rent multiple event venues throughout the metro area. Since these are not actually our spaces, we can't control everything we'd like to about each building's appearance. But even though there are things we can't change, we make sure we've done the best we can with what we have control over. We can't fix the cracks in the sidewalk out front, but we can sweep up the trash. Even if it is city trash from the day before, it becomes our responsibility if it poses the threat of hindering our guests' first impression.

Make no excuses when it comes to bringing the appearance of your space up to par. You can't do everything, but you can make sure that God's house—whether old or new, big or small, rented or owned—is presentable for the company he's expecting. Remember: *Everything speaks to first-time guests.*

The most critical part of the *greeted* area of initial contact is who your guests meet when they make it to the front door of the church—your greeters. A friendly face offering a warm welcome speaks volumes. Greeters should practically radiate the underlying message you want to send to your guests: *We are nice people, and we are glad you are here!* After first- or second-time guests visit The Journey, we encourage them to fill out short surveys about their first impressions. (We will examine these surveys and their usefulness a little later.) By far, one of the most common responses we get to the what-did-you-notice/what-made-you-want-to-return kind of questions references the people the guests met upon entering. Here's just one of the many we've recently received:

Q: What did you notice?
A: Smiling, friendly faces greeting us as we entered the building. A very positive experience!

As you put people in place as greeters, make sure they understand the importance of their job and know exactly what is expected of them. Volunteers need and want clear direction from you and your staff. They will feel more comfortable at their post if you've told them what you want them to say and how you want them to say it. Greeters, along with all volunteers, have an innate fear of not pleasing you, and at the same time you have a fear of asking too much of them. This creates a vicious cycle where everyone is tiptoeing around everyone else, and the guests aren't being greeted as effectively as they could be. At The Journey, our greeters know we expect them to smile, say "Hello!" and make sure each guest gets a program. The most important part of that job is the smile. (To access detailed job descriptions for your ushers and greeters, visit www.FusionBook.com.)

In a prominent Manhattan McDonald's, there's a sign that reads: "We expect all of our employees to smile at you. If you are not smiled at while your order is being taken, you get a free order of French fries or a free small drink." Why would McDonald's do that? Because they understand the undeniable power of a smile. According to one researcher:

> We can pick up a smile from thirty meters away. A smile lets us know that we are going to get a positive reception and it's hard not to reciprocate.[2]

A smile lightens the load of opposition and defenses that an unchurched person may be carrying through the door. But not just any smile—a genuine smile. A smile that doesn't engage the eyes is automatically interpreted as false. Great greeters are truly friendly people who make eye contact and offer sincere smiles.

Our volunteer system is a little different than most. We never know who is going to show up to help with the service on any given Sunday. We have developed a culture where our people always have the option of coming an hour early to serve, so every week we trust God that one to two hundred volunteers will show up—and they do. Once everyone arrives, we divide the responsibilities among them. We are intentional about making sure the friendliest people with the most genuine smiles are stationed as greeters. (For more on creating a culture where people are eager to serve, see my book *Connect: How to Double Your Number of Volunteers*.)

To choose our greeters, we have been known to do smile practice in our pre-service volunteer meeting. Not only does everyone get to practice putting on a huge smile, but the people who end up as greeters understand that the smile they give guests is so important that it just landed them the position. There's an old business axiom that says you can hire unfriendly people and work hard to teach them to smile or you can hire smiling, friendly people and turn them loose. The latter seems like a nice shortcut to us, which is why we think it's important to choose our greeters wisely instead of simply putting the first volunteers who show up in that position.

2. Directed

The second step in a successful pre-service is to make sure your guests are quickly, simply, and politely shown where they need to go, either by a sign or a volunteer—preferably by both. Imagine if Jon and Liz had walked through the door of FCC and had no idea where the restroom was. Since their child needed one, not only would they be facing a minor emergency, but they also would have been put in the awkward position of having to stop someone to ask. Automatically, this would have made Jon and Liz feel more uncomfortable and out of place. Their level of anxiety would have risen at the expense of their positive first impression. The same thing would happen if they didn't know where or how to drop off their kids for the children's ministry.

We all know the cultural importance of the phrase "location, location, location." Well, at church, the equally important phrase to remember is "signs, signs, signs"! Signs are the single best way to ensure that your guests can easily find what they need. Make sure you have clear signs pointing the way to:

- the restroom
- the children's area

These two areas in particular demand intentional signage. If your front door is not easily discernible from the parking lot, put a sign in place for it as well.

Again, it is easy to become so familiar with your surroundings that you become blind to them. The tendency is to think that your guests will "figure it out" and that your building is "pretty easy to navigate." For you, that's true. For your guests who have never set foot in your door and whose anxiety levels are already registering high, it's not. They have taken a big step by simply crossing the threshold into your church. Make sure you throw them the safety net of letting them know exactly where to go next. Even if you think you have enough signs, you probably don't.

In traveling to and working with thousands of churches, I am continually amazed at how difficult it is to navigate the average church building. Whether I'm arriving for a seminar or a service, I'm usually unclear on exactly where to park, where to enter the building, or how to find the main sanctuary—and I am generally very good with directions. If I find it difficult to navigate unfamiliar church buildings, unchurched people who are already anxious about the situation they are entering into certainly find church buildings confusing. And confusion creates anxiety. If your building is the least bit perplexing to your first-timers, they will become even more anxious than they already are. Good directions and an abundance of signage can lower their anxiety and lead them through the open door that leads to hearing the Good News.

Let your staff and greeters serve as backup to your signs. Train your staff and have them train your greeters to look for people who seem unsure of where to go, and to approach them and ask if they need help. If a guest asks for directions to a particular location, your staff person or greeter should never just point out the way. Instead, he or she should act as a personal escort. If it's to the children's ministry, your staff person or greeter may want to go so far as to introduce the new parents and children to whoever is in charge of the children's area. As the old saying goes, God is in the details.

3. Treated

First-time guests want to feel respected and welcomed. Guests want to know that you are happy they're there and that you are serious about making sure they have a good experience. The way you, your team, and your regular attenders treat guests and their families will tell them most of what they need to know. Sadly, a large majority of American churches aren't eager to welcome guests, much less make them feel at home. When guests show up, these churches have no idea what to do with them. We've all heard the stories about (or witnessed firsthand) first-time guests being altogether ignored or made to feel as if they were in the wrong place. What does that communicate about God's love? Do you think those guests would ever choose to return to such an environment? Or ever to step through the doors of another church again?

The church is not a business, but again, if we want to learn how to make our visitors feel welcome, we would be smart to take some cues from the customer-conscious service world. As we saw in the Ritz-Carlton example, businesses understand that treating guests with respect and making sure they have a good first experience is critical to winning a return visit. Shouldn't churches be the ones teaching the business world about embracing and serving those who walk through our doors?

This is where biblical hospitality meets the business concept of customer service. Unfortunately, we have all let the customer service aspect of our ministry slide for way too long. In Ken Blanchard's exploration of stellar customer service, *Raving Fans: A Revolutionary Approach to Customer Service*, he defines three secrets to creating environments that will wow your guests and make them feel appreciated. One of those secrets is to always *deliver your vision plus one percent*:[3]

> "Let's look at it," said Andrew. "The secret says two things. First, it tells you to deliver. Not sometimes, not most times, but all the time. Second it talks about 'plus one percent.' I'll come back to that, but first of all we have to talk about delivery."
>
> "Consistency, consistency, consistency," interjected Charlie. "Consistency is critical. Consistency creates credibility. My pro will explain how it works. Andrew, if you please."
>
> "With pleasure, Charlie," said Andrew. "As Charlie told you, consistency is key to delivering Raving Fan Service. When you're creating Raving Fans, it's a fragile relationship. They've been burned before and don't trust easily. You're trying to pull them in and they're usually trying to resist. Consistency will overcome resistance, but in the meantime, they're watching like a hawk for you to mess up."[4]

How true this is in your attempt to create Raving Fans out of first-time guests. Most of the people who walk through your door have been burned by the church, by negative press about the church, or by a friend or family member in the name of religion. More than likely, they are skeptical and waiting, as Andrew suggested, for you to mess up. When you give them a consistent pre-service experience that makes them feel valued, their skepticism lowers as their positive impression and curiosity rises, leaving you in the perfect position to make a real impact. And how do you continually add the one percent that makes their experience just a little sweeter? Well, food isn't associated with comfort and pleasure for nothing.

The late food writer James Beard once said, "Food is our common ground, a universal experience."[5] It also provides a welcome, comforting treat in any situation. A warm cup of coffee at the office acts as a security blanket for millions of adults every day. Ever notice how a two-hundred-pound man in a crowd of strangers suddenly feels more comfortable if he has an eight-ounce Styrofoam cup to hide behind? Providing food is one of the best ways to show your guests you care about them, and it's a sure way to put them at ease.

When done well, food can go a long way toward wowing your guests, but when done poorly, it really turns them off. A few words of advice: don't skimp on food. This is not the area to try to save a nickel. Don't cut things in half to make them stretch. Don't glare at the person who takes three donuts. Food is your chance to show unchurched people that you care enough to offer them something for free that will meet a need.

Food is certainly not a necessity, but we've found that it goes a long way toward making a solid impression. If you choose to do it, do it well. Keep in mind that you aren't preparing a five-course breakfast. You are simply making your food offering with excellence. Quality, not extravagance, is the key.

Recently, we received this survey response from a first-time guest—and we hear echoes of this sentiment each and every week:

Q: What did you notice?
A: The smiles, warm reception, and Krispy Kreme donuts.

Q: What did you like best?
A: Besides the friendly and casual atmosphere, the coffee and donuts!

4. Seated

Now that your guests have been sincerely greeted, helpfully directed, and well treated, all that's left is for them to be properly seated. While it would be easy to let your guests fend for themselves to find a seat, it's a terrible idea. Think back to Jon and Liz. As they started timidly down the aisle, if no volunteer had popped up to show them to their seats, they would have walked nervously by filled rows, looking for empty seats, hoping they wouldn't have to squeeze past someone already seated. They probably would have ended up close to the back of the church, where they could more easily find empty spaces without having to interact with anyone and where they wouldn't have to truly engage with the worship service.

Thankfully the aisle usher, who was ready and eager to escort them to seats, relieved Jon and Liz of the pressure they were starting to feel. The usher could ask those already seated to slide toward the middle or to stand and let Jon and Liz slide in, which the two of them would never do on their own. So Jon and Liz ended up in comfortable seats, close to the front, without fumbling through any anxiety-inducing situations.

The first time my wife and I went to a Broadway show, we saw the value of a good usher in action. From the moment we entered the theater, we were literally ushered to our seats. If you've ever experienced Broadway, you know the drill: the usher who scans your ticket points you toward the correct entrance, where there is another usher who points you toward the correct aisle, where there is yet another usher who walks you directly to your row and motions to your seats. In that first Broadway experience, we knew that as long as we had our ticket in hand for the ushers to see, they would do all the work. We were along for the ride. That's usher service. On the other hand, we've been to sporting events and concert venues where we missed the first fifteen minutes because we were still trying to find the correct wing, level, section, and row that would lead us to our seats. We were on our own, juggling concession purchases and upset that we were missing something we had paid to see. There was certainly no usher in place to make sure we had a smooth experience.

Here's the difference in thinking: those Broadway shows run every night. They want you to come again. They want you to tell your friends. They want you to bring out-of-town guests. They want to ensure you've had an experience that will keep you coming back for more. At most concerts and special events, the venue proprietors aren't nearly as concerned with earning your repeat business. They know that the draw is that night's particular entertainment. The next night their guests will be a new, differently focused crowd who will be there to see their favorite artist or team, generally in spite of venue conditions. Earning a return visit through impressing with a high level of service is not a priority to them.

When it comes to providing service to our first-time guests, we need to stay aware that our goal is to make them as comfortable and happy as possible. We want them to come back. We want them to bring their friends. Let's approach this area of service with the mind-set of Broadway's bright lights rather than that of self-service stadiums.

The thinking behind *greeted*, *directed*, *treated*, and *seated* may be a paradigm shift for you. Until this point, your plan for first-time guests may have been simply to get them through the door and make your impression with the service itself. While that sounds good in theory, research has shown that you don't have that luxury. By the time your service starts, your guests have already made judgments about your environment, interacted with people who may or may not have rubbed them the right way, figured out how to navigate your hallways, and found themselves a seat—more than enough experience with your church for that gut-level feeling to have firmly formed. And once the first impression has been made, you can do very little in the service to change it.

What's more, if they have formed a negative first impression, that impression becomes the lens through which they view everything else in the service. They become closed to the worship you've worked so hard to plan and to the message you've prepared for them. Conversely, if you create Raving Fans in the pre-service, they will engage in the rest of your service with a heightened sense of enthusiasm, which leaves them more open to hearing from God.

In his instruction to the church at Corinth, Paul encouraged his listeners to "let all things be done decently and in order" (1 Cor. 14:40 NKJV). Why? Because everything done in a church service works together to represent God's character to unchurched people. They may not immediately know why they like your church or why they feel comfortable, but it's because you've done the work to set them at ease. You have established an environment that resonates positively with their subconscious mind before they even begin to evaluate that environment on a conscious level.

Something in them connects with the smile they've been offered. They feel relief that they don't have to ask for directions to the restroom. They feel loved by the donuts and coffee you've made available to them. They appreciate the seats you've provided. In the first seven minutes, all of these things work together to create an impression that will open the door of opportunity for you to minister in their lives in a truly meaningful way. With a strong pre-service in place, seven minutes is all you need to show your guests just how much you care about them and want them back.

4

making contact

The art of communication is the language of leadership.

James Humes

Live wisely among those who are not believers, and make the most of every opportunity.

Apostle Paul (Col. 4:5)

We have all heard, "Build it and they will come." Well, maybe they will. But whether or not they'll leave a calling card is another question altogether—one that depends largely on you. In his letters, Paul offers insight into reaching and keeping unchurched guests. He instructs:

Live wisely among those who are not believers, and **make the most of every opportunity.** (Col. 4:5, emphasis added)

What do you suppose "make the most of every opportunity" looks like in relation to your first-time guests? Of course it means greeting them with a strong pre-service, as we've learned. But that's not all.

Making the most of every opportunity also means being intentional about getting what you need to be able to contact your first-timers after the service is over. Without your guests' contact information, you have no hope of assimilating them. That doesn't mean you tackle them at the door if they don't sign your registry. Such extreme measures won't be necessary if you put an information-gathering system in place that will make them feel comfortable giving you their basic contact information. Yes, it is possible to make guests completely willing, and even eager, to give you their personal information. Imagine that! But if you don't make the most of your first opportunity to do so, you probably won't get another shot.

Without contact information, the Fusion assimilation system breaks down. So once your first-time guests have successfully made it from the street to the seat, getting their information should be one of your primary goals—not just inspiring them with beautiful music or impacting them with your preaching. Your focus should not only be on getting them to respond to an invitation but also on knowing how to invite them back so that they can witness the power of God in a consistent way.

Please don't misunderstand me. God can certainly use your service to bring first-time guests to saving knowledge.

However, guests who set foot inside a church for the first time and leave completely transformed by the Spirit are the exception, not the rule. Unchurched people usually need more than a single exposure to God's truth and the power of his love before they start becoming receptive to its meaning for them. That's why it is incredibly important for you to make them feel welcome and ensure that you know how to follow up with them and invite them back to your church.

So what's the best way to get your guests' information? How can you find out what you need to know without coming across as intrusive and pushy? In working with all types of churches, I have seen countless plans in place, each used with varying degrees of success: check-in at the front door, books passed down the aisles, reception tables after the service, and nametags, among others. Some of these have merit, but there's one method that experience continues to prove successful time and time again: the Connection Card. Well-organized use of Connection Cards (or Communication Cards, as they are sometimes called) will allow you to gather the information you need on over 80 percent of your first-time guests. Eighty percent is a great return in most any endeavor, but it is surprisingly great when it comes to getting personal information from unchurched people.

The Connection Card

(Or, The One Thing You Want Everyone to Do)

The Connection Card is just that—a card that enables you to connect with every person who attends your church on a given Sunday. Measuring about a third of a page, the

Connection Card is printed on card stock and inserted into the program. Don't stick it in the back of the chairs or pews. Put it in the program, and put the program in the hand of each guest who comes through the door. This is the best way to ensure that no one is overlooked. Here's a tip: also pass out pens with your programs. Remove all stumbling blocks.

Once everyone who has entered your church has a Connection Card–bearing program in his or her hand, the process of information gathering can begin. Let's see how the use of the Connection Card plays out for Jon and Liz at FCC.

After standing through a few worship songs, Jon and Liz, intrigued yet slightly uncomfortable, are relieved when finally instructed to take their seats. A man in his midforties steps onto the platform and introduces himself.

"Welcome to FCC," he says enthusiastically. "I'm Tim, one of FCC's teaching pastors. You've picked a great day to be here! Today we are starting a brand-new series, 'Life 360.' Before we jump in, take a moment and look inside your program where you'll find an FCC Connection Card. Go ahead and pull that out. If you are a regular attender or a member, please fill in your name and email address. If you are a first-time guest with us today, welcome! We are excited that you chose today to check out FCC for the first time. We'd like to ask you to take the next few moments to fill out as much information as you feel comfortable sharing on the front of your Connection Card. You can drop your card in the offering bucket as it passes by at the end of the service."

Jon glances around the room and notices that everyone is doing what Tim asked. On both sides of him, people are busy filling out the little cards. He figures he better do the same if he hopes to remain incognito. Jon checks his pocket for a pen and then remembers the one he was handed as he came in. He pulls out the card and quickly fills in his name, email address, and home address. He has played along, but he's not sure whether or not he'll actually turn in the card at the end of the service. He's not big on the idea of being put on some kind of church mailing list.

Jon and Liz engage in the rest of the service with a kind of reserved curiosity. He's never gotten much out of church before, but a couple of the points Tim brings up register with him. Slightly surprised at his own behavior, Jon finds himself jotting down notes. As the teaching draws to a close, Tim goes back to the Connection Card.

"Go ahead and pull your Connection Card out again and look at the back. You'll see a list of possible Next Steps you can take following today's message. Maybe you'd like to memorize this week's verse or commit to being here through the rest of this series. Just check the box to let us know. If you'd like more information on FCC's small groups, member-ship, or baptism, just check the appropriate box, and we'll be sure to get that information to you. If we can be praying for you in a specific way, write that on the lines provided, and know that you will be prayed for this week."

Jon glances over and is a little annoyed to see Liz check-ing off boxes for more information. He gives her a quizzi-cal glare and wonders if she's really planning on turning in the card.

"Now," Tim continues, "if you are a first-time guest, we'd like to offer you a free gift. Just drop your Connection Card in the offering bucket as it's passed, and you can pick up your free copy of *Unshakable* by Nelson Searcy on your way out." (For your own free copy of my book *Unshakable: Standing Strong When Things Go Wrong*, visit www .FusionBook.com.)

Liz grins knowingly in Jon's direction. He's a reader and can never turn down a free book—especially one that may help him make sense of, maybe even disprove, all of this faith talk. With the offering bucket coming toward him, Jon starts reasoning with himself: *Maybe the junk mail wouldn't be so bad. Probably wouldn't be much of it. And it would actually be interesting to keep up with what's going on around this place. After all, that book looks like a good one, and I can't take a copy without dropping in the card.*

Suddenly finding the bucket in his hand, Jon drops in his Connection Card. Liz does the same. Passing it on, Jon puts his arm around Liz's shoulders and wonders if there are any Krispy Kremes left in the back.

Knowing how to structure the use of the Connection Card for maximum impact is critical to your guests' future. It is far more critical to their future than to yours. This process is not about you. It's about giving your guests the best possible opportunity to step out of their comfort zone and turn over closely held information.

Why? Not so that you can add to the numbers, but so that you can follow up with them in a way that will make them want to keep connecting with the church for their own spiritual development. This is about them and how you can help them move from unchurched visitors to fully developing followers of Jesus Christ. Knowing that, you have to be willing, once again, to look at the scenario through their eyes. What will make your guests most comfortable giving you information? What will make them actually want to give you information? How can you keep them from being skeptical and let them know that you truly have their best interests at heart?

How to Use the Connection Card

In the classic work *How to Win Friends and Influence People*, Dale Carnegie gives every effective leader guidelines to keep in mind when trying to influence another's attitude and behavior. And make no mistake, when you are dealing with unchurched individuals in a structured church setting, you have to change their attitude and predisposed behavior before they will willingly give you anything. If you were in their place, wouldn't you be hesitant? To overcome the reticence of others, Carnegie suggests the following:

- Be sincere. Do not promise anything you cannot deliver. Forget about the benefits to yourself and concentrate on the benefits to the other person.
- Know exactly what it is you want the other person to do.
- Be empathetic. Ask yourself what it is the other person really wants.
- Consider the benefits that person will receive from doing what you suggest.
- Match those benefits to the other person's wants.
- When you make your request, put it in a form that will convey to the other person the idea that he personally will benefit.[1]

Each one of the principles Carnegie outlines can be directly applied to your Connection Card. Your guests need to know that you sincerely want to serve them. Their experience in your pre-service will likely determine whether they believe the sincerity of your motives. They need to have a clear description of what you want them to do and when, and they should get this information from your announcement. They need to know that you understand that they don't want to be singled out in any way. They need to see personal benefit in doing what you ask and know that they will get something they want—information and maybe a free gift—out of following your instruction.

Keeping Jon and Liz's experience in mind, let's break down the successful use of a Connection Card.

1. Everyone Fills Out a Card Every Week

Guests don't want to be singled out. One of the surest ways to make them self-conscious and uncomfortable is to differentiate them from the crowd. If you do that, their emotional defenses will rise—which is the exact opposite of what you want. If you are hoping to connect with the unchurched, you have to keep their anxiety and defenses in check.

Most unchurched individuals stay that way because they don't think they can visit a service anonymously. They are afraid they'll have attention drawn to them by having to stand and say their name or participate in some other welcoming ritual. Knowing that fear of public speaking ranks higher in psychological studies than the fear of death, why do so many churches still ask their guests to address a crowd of strangers? Don't do anything to bring unwanted attention to those visiting your church. Guests prefer to be practically invisible—and that means not asking them to do anything that everyone else isn't doing. Instead, provide them with a Connection Card in their program and a pen when they walk through the door, and then encourage them to fill out their card when it's time.

Over the years, we have developed a Connection Card script that, once ingrained into a church's culture—which usually takes about six months—consistently gets over 80 percent of a crowd to fill out a Connection Card. (For a downloadable version of the Connection Card script, go to www.FusionBook.com.) I encourage you to study this script and then put it to work for you:

Good morning and welcome to *[church name]*. My name is *[name]*—I'm the pastor of *[area]* here at *[church name]*, and I'm so glad you've joined us today as we continue our *[series name]* teaching series. In just a few moments, Pastor *[name of the day's teaching pastor]* is going to be out here to share a message all about *[message topic]*. It's going to be a great day!

But first, I'd like to draw your attention to the program you should have received when you came in today. Inside that program is a Connection Card that looks just like this. *[Hold up card.]*

If you haven't done so already, will you take the pen we gave you and begin filling out this card? If you're a regular attender or a member, you can just give us your name and email address and any information that may have changed. *[Pause.]*

But if this is your first time with us, I'd like to ask you to complete as much information as you feel comfortable sharing . . . and be sure to mark the box on the left-hand side that says "First-" or "Second-Time Guest." *[Pause.]*

As you work your way down the card, you'll see a question at the bottom that says "How did you hear about [church name]?" As a church that cares about this community, you can probably imagine that we're interested in how you found out about us—so I'd really appreciate that valuable information. [Bigger pause.]

Now, one of the main reasons we ask everyone—and I mean everyone—to fill out the front of this card is because we believe that God has an important next step for you to take on the back of this card. And when you fill out the front of this card, you're putting yourself in a position to take one of these important Next Steps. So go ahead and turn over to the back of your Connection Card now. [Turn your card over.] You'll find a number of Next Steps. There's a lot of great stuff going on here at [church name].

Pastor [name of the day's teaching pastor] will share more Next Steps with you during today's message, so hang on to your Connection Card and we'll collect them during the offering at the end of the service.

Having everyone fill out a Connection Card each week serves a number of purposes. First of all, guests feel more comfortable doing what you've asked them to do because they aren't alone. If you asked just the guests to fill out a card, they would be hesitant to do so because that would announce to the world that they are, in fact, guests. Plus, as we saw with Jon, the peer pressure aspect of a congregation-wide activity actually encourages guests to participate—they won't be singled out by not playing along. Second, by having both your regular attenders and members fill out the Connection Card, you will have a record of their attendance, a way for your regular attenders to take spiritual Next Steps (more on Next Steps in chapter 6), and a way to keep track of changes in contact information. We suggest including a box for regular attenders to check if their contact information has changed so that you know whose information needs to be updated each week without cross-checking every card.

The most powerful word for change in your church is *because*. When we first implemented the Connection Card at The Journey, we had a hard time getting our regular attenders and members to fill it out every week. Since we already knew their names and information, they saw it as a waste of time and effort. So we started using a few minutes in each Membership Class to let them know the method behind the madness. We explained that by having everyone in the church do the same thing at the same time, guests were more likely to go along and give us their much-needed information. But if guests could look around and spot others not filling out the card or others finishing too quickly (which is what would happen if you only asked regular attenders for their name), the chances of getting information from those guests dropped significantly. Of course, once they understood the rationale, almost everyone was on board. Our regular attenders and members have a heart for reaching the unchurched who come through our doors and they don't want to do anything that may hinder someone from making a trip back. When they understood the *why*, the *what* became a nonissue.

Make sure your Connection Card is simple, easy to read, and easy to fill out. If you are asking for an email address, provide a line long enough to hold a lengthy address. Don't frustrate your guests by asking for something and then making it hard for them to give it to you. Keep the card simple. You only need the necessities.

Notice that we don't ask for the date. We used to, but here's what we discovered about men: if they don't know the answer to the first question, they probably won't fill out the card at all. And on a Sunday, many people don't know the date off the top of their heads. This is not a pop quiz. Keep it to the point. Also, at this stage of your relationship, there is no need to ask for details such as children's ages, birthdays, and the like. Asking for too much information will make unchurched people skeptical and give them an excuse to chuck the idea altogether. You can get all of that information down the line in Membership Class. When it comes to having their information for follow-up, keep the main thing the main thing.

Deciding what that main thing is depends on your culture. At The Journey, we emphasize the email address and don't put much weight on getting a telephone number. We know our crowd, and a telephone call from the church would terrify most of them. Plus, given the fact that our demographic is extremely email compatible, that's the best way for us to go. If you are dealing with a less technological crowd or an older crowd, an email address could be irrelevant to you. Go for the phone number. The key is to know who you are dealing with and to keep things simple and easy. Your goal is to make all guests so comfortable filling out the Connection Card that they don't think twice about it. No guest should be left behind. (For a downloadable version of an effective Connection Card, visit www.FusionBook.com.)

2. Everyone Has a Next Step to Take

People are much more likely to do what you want them to do if they are happy about doing it. And if they become directly involved in and see personal benefit from doing what you ask, they'll be happy. Most people will give you what you want if they think they'll get something they want in return. That's just human nature. They are also more likely to engage with you when you are challenging them to take an action step. Perhaps it's cultural, but if we are asked what our next step is going to be in any scenario, we will identify one. Rarely will we let the question slide.

Next Steps on the back of the Connection Card challenge guests, regular attenders, and members to respond to the message in a tangible way. Some of the Next Steps relate specifically to what has just been taught. For example, if the message is on forgiveness, a Next Step might be to write down the name of someone you need to forgive and commit to reaching out to that person the following week. Some of the Next Steps are more general in nature, such as a commitment to memorize the memory verse or read a specific passage during the week. Still other Next Steps are more informational in nature, like a request for more information on a ministry opportunity, church membership, or baptism. Ideally, there will be at least one Next Step that jumps out at everyone. (For downloadable samples of what the back of my current Connection Card looks like, visit www.FusionBook.com.)

Guests are most likely to check one of the informational Next Steps, which is a direct invitation for you to follow up with them in a specific way. For purposes of gathering contact information, the important thing to remember is that extending the challenge to accept some sort of Next Step entices your guests to action. And if they've been compelled to check one of those boxes on the back of the Connection

Card, they'll be more likely to drop the card in the offering bucket when given the chance.

By throwing down the gauntlet and inviting them to action, you have personalized the message. You have helped them recognize that their response to what they've heard is important, and you've underscored the fact that you are interested in their individual needs. When they accept the challenge of marking a Next Step, they will want you to know it. Most guests will drop the card in the bucket, not wanting to end the dialogue you are inviting them into. If none of the Next Steps are enough enticement, offering a free gift usually is. Again, we will go into more detail about the role a free gift plays later, but for now let's take a quick look at its usefulness in helping you gather contact information.

Just before the offering bucket is passed at the end of the service (more on that in the next point), we like to thank our first-time guests once more for coming and give them a little extra incentive to turn in their Connection Card. We let them know a free gift is available for them on their way out. All they need to do to get it is drop their Connection Card in the offering bucket. As we make this announcement, we show them a picture of the gift—a copy of my book *Unshakable: Standing Strong When Things Go Wrong*—on the projection screens. Who doesn't like to get something for free? Especially if it's something that is of benefit to them, which is where the importance of understanding your demographic comes into play once again. Say something along the lines of this:

> In just a moment we are going to receive the offering, so please take this time to finish completing any information or Next Steps on your Connection Card, and you can finish

preparing your offering envelope if you came prepared to give financially today.

But first, I'd like to speak to those of you who are here for the very first time. We are so glad that you joined us, and in exchange for your completed Connection Card, we have a special gift for you. It's a book called *Unshakable* and it's all about how you can stand strong when things go wrong.

All you need to do is drop your completed Connection Card in the offering bucket with your offering when it's passed in a moment, then—after you've dropped your completed Connection Card in the bucket—swing by the "First-Time Guest" table just outside the exit doors on your way out. That's our way of saying thanks for joining us today.

Whatever you offer as a free gift, make sure it's something that the typical unbeliever visiting your church will see value in, and try to make it something that will encourage people to dig deeper into their examination of faith. Also, don't be greedy with the gift. We've found that it is best to stack a large supply of books on a table by the door and trust first-time guests to take one rather than having someone staff the table and ask, "Are you a first-time guest?" Make the process quick, anonymous, and painless. (For more on ordering bulk copies of *Unshakable* as free gifts for your first-time guests, go to www.FusionBook.com.)

3. Everyone Places His or Her Card in with the Offering

For the Connection Card to work like it should, you have to receive the offering at the end of the service. For some of you, this may be quite a break in tradition. It was for me. I come from a church background where the offering was received before the preaching, as is common in many churches. However, after studying the success of the system, I knew I couldn't let old habits stand in the way of bringing more people into the kingdom. I may have had to deal with some mixed-up priorities on my part, but I quickly learned that a sense of tradition should never stand in the way of changes that lead to effectiveness.

For your church to grow, you must continually ask yourself how you can be doing things better. Be quick to step back, evaluate where you are, and make changes that will help you get where God wants you to be. If shifting the order of your service seems drastic to you, measure it against the effectiveness of your current assimilation system. How many of your first-time guests are leaving you the information you need or engaging you in a dialogue? If you give them a chance to respond to your message, challenge them to a Next Step after the preaching, and then make it easy for them to turn in their card by combining it with the offering, I can guarantee a sharp increase in your rate of assimilation. If that means changing an ingrained habit, it's well worth it.

Effectively using Connection Cards is key to a healthy assimilation system. If this area fails, your assimilation system itself fails. Of course, God will bring some of your guests back on their own, but he has called you to the ministry of your church for a reason. A large part

Tradition should never stand in the way of changes that lead to effectiveness.

of that ministry is knowing how to do your part to keep the people he sends you as you trust him to stir their hearts. Too many schools of thought justify inactivity or lack of preparation by invoking God's sovereignty. Grabbing onto such an indisputable point as their excuse leaves them with little challenge and helps perpetuate a church culture of mediocrity. When leaders attribute failure to the will of God, despite the fact that they may have completely disregarded their own God-given responsibility in the inner workings of that failure, they discredit God's will.

You and I have been called to plant and water so that God can grow the harvest—and not to plant and water haphazardly, but to the best of our abilities as we are laboring for his kingdom. We must do the work to ensure a connection with our guests. God promises us that if we step toward him, he will step toward us (see James 4:8).

5

creating fans
through follow-up

Not following up . . . is the same as filling up
your bathtub without first putting the stopper
in the drain.

David Frey

Come, be my disciples, and I will show you how
to fish for people!

Jesus (Mark 1:17)

Tim dismisses the crowd and Liz begins gathering her things.

"Hurry," Jon says. "Let's get out of here before we have
to talk to anyone."

"Don't you want to say hi to Sam?" asks Liz.

"No need," says Jon. "I'll see him in the morning." *By that time*, Jon thinks to himself, *I'll have had a chance to make some sense of this place. If we run into Sam now, we'll inevitably have to be introduced to his church friends and won't get out of here for another half hour.*

"You go get the kids," Jon says to Liz. "I'll pull the car around to the front."

"Don't forget that free book," Liz calls as he walks away.

Did she really think he would? Jon grabs two copies of *Unshakable* on his way out the door—one for himself and one for Liz. With the books tucked under his arm and the message notes still in his hand, Jon rushes to the car.

Pulling the door closed behind him, he flips the radio to the baseball game, puts the car in gear, and eases toward the entrance. No sign of Liz and the kids yet. What could be taking them so long?

"Strike two!" blares the radio commentator. Glancing around the parking lot and then at his watch, Jon grabs one of the books he's thrown on Liz's seat as the pitcher winds up again. Opening the book, he notices a folded piece of paper stuck in the middle.

"Ball! One more of those and he'll walk, Joe." Jon turns the radio down a notch and pulls out the paper. It's a letter. As he starts to scan it, the back door swings open.

"Daddy! We drew you a picture today!"

"Really? Let me see!" And to Liz, "What took you so long?"

"Sorry. We stopped by the guest table to pick up a few things." She lays a couple of brochures and a CD on the dashboard. "Met the pastor, too. Nice guy. I think you'd like him. Who's winning?"

Speaking of baseball, have you ever played? How about golf? Both of these games exemplify the power of follow-up—or in sports vernacular, follow-through. What if a baseball batter or a golfer stopped swinging as soon as he made contact with the ball? It wouldn't go anywhere, right? The ball would simply drop to the ground. There would be no momentum to drive it forward, no power to propel it. You may be thinking: *That's ridiculous! In a sports swing, you have to follow through. The inertia gained in the first part of your swing demands it.*

Exactly.

Baseball players and golfers cannot help but follow through on the force of their contact. It happens almost automatically—a result of sheer momentum. What's the lesson? Follow-through is not optional; it's integral. However, the health of that follow-through, the precision and form of it, will determine where and just how far the ball actually goes every time. The same truth applies to your follow-up.

Contact with the ball happens as your guests drop their cards in the offering. Your follow-up swing begins the moment of your final "Amen." How can you hone your momentum and guarantee effectiveness? By implementing a follow-up strategy that will show your appreciation for your guests' visit and entice them to join you again.

There are three things to keep in mind as you seek to create a follow-up strategy that will bring your guests back. I like to refer to them as the three *F*'s of follow-up:

1. Follow up *fast*. Don't underestimate the power of a quick follow-up. There is a new expectation for immediacy in our world.
2. Be *friendly*. Your follow-up needs to reach out to your guests in a warm, personal way. Make them feel valued as individuals rather than sending them something that resembles a mass form mailing.
3. Make your follow-up *functional*. Follow up with your guests in a way that meets them where they are. Convey your information in a simple and straightforward manner, take the opportunity to invite them back, and provide them with a life-relevant surprise.

A successful *fast*, *friendly*, and *functional* follow-up system exists in two phases: post-service follow-up and post-weekend follow-up.

Post-service Follow-Up

Your post-service follow-up consists of the free gift you offer your first-timers and what you make available to them at your guest table.

Free Gift

As we saw in the last chapter, offering a free gift—preferably a free book—not only encourages your first-time guests to turn in their contact information, but also gives you the powerful opportunity to surprise them with something that can help them on their spiritual journey. There is a third important reason the free gift is part of an effective assimilation system: offering a free gift provides you with the perfect opportunity to begin your follow-up.

When one of our guests picks up *Unshakable*, there is a letter from me tucked inside that thanks them for coming to The Journey and invites them to visit our website to fill out a first-time guest survey and get more information about the church. (For more on creating an online guest survey, visit www.FusionBook .com.) So if someone chooses not to turn in their Connection Card but still takes a book on the way out, we haven't missed the opportunity to do a little bit of follow-up with them.

> **The Three *F*'s of Follow-Up**
>
> 1. Fast
> 2. Friendly
> 3. Functional

To be effective, the free gift that you put in the hands of your first-time guests should do three things:

- Remind them of their experience at your church
- Cause them to think about where they stand with God
- Give them a ready-made invitation to seek out more information

When a guest at our church receives a copy of *Unshakable*, we have confidence that—if he or she will take the time to engage with it—the book will be instrumental either in leading that person to Jesus or into a deeper relationship with him. There's nothing wrong with giving free mugs, fresh-baked bread, or any other number of gifts, but if that's your choice, you should also give something along with that gift that will help lead the people you have an opportunity to influence closer to God. A free book is the ideal option.

Unshakable: Standing Strong When Things Go Wrong is a book that connects with both believers and with unchurched people in a unique way. Set up as a topical guidebook, it addresses the wide range of storms we all face in life. Rather than reading *Unshakable* straight through—something many unchurched people would be hesitant to do with any book they receive at church—readers can simply flip to the issue they currently need direction on and find hope and help in one short chapter. *Unshakable* tackles many of the issues your first-time guests are likely to be wrestling with:

- financial stress
- failure
- marital issues
- death
- lack of purpose
- disconnection from God
- doubt
- illness
- career challenges
- temptation
- family problems

No matter what your guests are walking through, *Unshakable* will meet them where they are and point them to the hope Jesus offers through and on the other side of their storm.

Since its original publication, *Unshakable* has proven to be an indispensable tool with first-time guests both at The Journey and at many other churches across the country. Since every person who picks up the book will eventually face most of the difficulties it addresses, *Unshakable* is not only relevant immediately but it also becomes a go-to guide for years to come—and a continual reminder of your church's invitation to connect on a deeper level. (For more information on using *Unshakable* as a free gift for your first-time guests, go to www.FusionBook.com.)

On big Sundays, such as Christmas or Easter, consider adding a little something extra to the free gift. We have been known to put movie tickets or ice-cream gift cards inside the books. Never underestimate the power of wowing your guests.

The unchurched first-timers who walk through our doors are usually steeped in the *every man for himself* mind-set so prevalent in our society—they are not used to being cared about by strangers and certainly are not used to getting something for nothing. That's why so many of them have a hardened heart toward Jesus's message. His sacrifice doesn't make sense in their reality. If we can show them even in small, seemingly insignificant ways that we want to serve them without anything in return, they will begin to see the reflection of God's love through that service.

Guest Table

Some of your guests will not be in as much of a hurry to duck out as Jon was. They may want to ask some questions, get more information on specific ministries, and meet you or some of your staff. The most effective way to give them that opportunity is to designate a clearly marked guest table. During your closing remarks, mention that the table is available for anyone who has questions or would like to pick up additional information.

At The Journey, I or one of the other pastors stands by the guest table at the end of each service to talk with the guests who stop by. I am not manning the table or forcing everyone to shake my hand. Rather, I'm making myself available next to it. Always have a friendly, knowledgeable volunteer in charge of the table itself.

Many people ask me why we choose to use a guest table instead of a guest reception room. In our culture, people are on the run. Most of them grab their free gift and maybe a little information, and then they are out the door. The idea of mingling in a social environment, even if only for five or ten minutes, is both constraining and intimidating to them. I don't ever want curious guests to leave without getting desired information because they were hesitant to go into a small room and mingle with other guests.

Psychology tells us that a significant number of people will avoid such a social scenario out of shyness or fear alone. I would rather provide a place where they can pick up the information they need on their own terms. If they want to ask questions of the volunteer or linger and talk with me, they are more than welcome to. If not, they are under no pressure or obligation and can still get the information they want. Providing a simple table takes away potential obstacles and allows guests to take advantage of what you are offering in whatever way they feel most comfortable.

Post-weekend Follow-Up

Come Monday, Jon is back in his regular routine. He's buried in emails most of the morning before heading into the weekly staff meeting. He sees Sam in the meeting.

"Hey, Jon," says Sam. "Saw you across the way yesterday morning. I tried to find you after the service."

"Yeah, we had to run. Afternoon plans."

"That's what I figured. No big deal. What did you think of our church?"

Before Jon has a chance to answer, the meeting is called to order.

By lunchtime, Jon is, as usual, ready to get out of the office and read for a few minutes. Only today, he's not reading the standard market-trend fare. Instead, he heads outside with his sandwich in one hand and *Unshakable* in the other.

Later that day, around 3:00 p.m., Jon's email bings. He opens it, surprised to find an email from Tim at FCC.

36-Hour Email Response

Monday is the greatest day of the week when it comes to your post-weekend follow-up. Don't wait to get the follow-up going. Have you ever given someone a gift and gotten a thank-you note almost immediately? Doesn't that make you feel acknowledged and appreciated? Remember that your guests are gifts, and they gave part of their weekend to you. If you take the time to connect with them the next day, they will start to see that they are a priority with you even after the service is over. The positive emotion you'll create by showing them how much you valued their attendance will go a long way toward bringing them back for a second visit.

Within a day and a half after their visit, each and every one of your first-time guests should receive an email that

(1) thanks them for attending your church and (2) invites them to come back. Make sure you do both of these things. Too often, churches thank their guests for attending but fail to give them a direct invitation to return.

At The Journey, this email also gives guests a direct link to the first-time guest survey on our website. The link provides them with a one-click opportunity to share their thoughts on their experience and to get more information about the church. Keep in mind that this may not work exactly the same way for your demographic. Our crowd is 100 percent email savvy. That's the number one way we can get them to communicate with us. You may need to tweak the system to fit your needs. As a sidenote, we also send texts to the people who provide cell phone numbers. While email is definitely the most effective 36-hour response, it is also wise to use the cell phone number for follow-up, if you can get it.

Each week, the correspondence that goes out—both the emails and the personal notes (as you'll see below)—are signed by the teaching pastor who spoke that Sunday. If I didn't teach, my name is not the name on the note. Your guests will remember and relate to the person who gave the message.

Subject: Great to see you at The Journey!

From: [Your name (or name of the pastor who taught on Sunday, if not you)]

Hey [first name],

I had an open moment and wanted to shoot you a quick email to let you know it was great to have you at The Journey on Sunday—hope your first experience was meaningful and enjoyable.

Would you do me a favor?

Because it's important to us that you felt welcomed and had a positive experience your first time at The Journey, would you take a few seconds to fill out a quick online survey for me? (It will only take about thirty seconds.)

[web address]

Or just reply to this email and let me know your thoughts.

If there is anything I can do for you, or if there is a specific way that I can be praying for you . . . please feel free to let me know.

I'll be in touch again soon.

[your name]

P.S. I've attached a picture of my family, and here are a few bits of info:

1. My name is [first name], and my wife's name is [first name]. We have been married for [number] years!

2. We have a son named [first name] (born in [year])—you'll see him running around Journey Kidz on Sundays.

3. My wife and I are longtime bulldog owners, but right now we are "in between," so our house is currently dog hair–free.

4. Before moving here, I pastored on the Upper West Side of Manhattan for ten years. I'm still looking for a great NYC cheesecake around here. Let me know if you have a recommendation!

———————

[your name]

[your title, church name]

[web address]

Check out The Journey on Facebook:

[web address]

The 36-Hour Email Response is almost the same in content as the letter we put in the free copies of *Unshakable*, plus an intentional postscript that's meant to make a personal connection. Sending this email accomplishes three things: (1) it follows up on those who did not take a book or read the letter; (2) it lets guests know we are thinking about them the next day; and (3) it invites them to give us feedback and explore the website for more insight into the church.

Through lots of trial and error, we have found that between 2:00 p.m. and 3:00 p.m. on Monday afternoon is the best time to send your follow-up email. The open rate on Monday mornings is not nearly as high. Most people don't check their email on Sunday and have so many emails on Monday morning that your follow-up could easily get lost in the shuffle or pushed to the trash. But by 2:00 p.m. or 3:00 p.m., people are caught up and even looking for a little distraction from their Monday routine. The online survey is a perfect distraction.

You will notice that we do not ask any questions that require a critique of our church. Our goal here is not to reinforce any negative experience they may have had. We've found that if something is really bad, they will tell us in the overall impression question. This doesn't mean we don't want discerning feedback—we do. We simply prefer to elicit the more critical feedback from our second-time guests, as you will see in the next chapter.

"I'm home," Jon calls, as he walks in the front door with the mail in his hand. It's Thursday evening and he's ready for another weekend. Still no plans, unless you count yard work. Liz walks in from the den to meet him.

"Hey. Good day?"

"I guess." Flipping through bills and credit-card offers, he comes across a smaller envelope with his and Liz's name and address handwritten on the front. Liz spots it too.

"Who's that from?" she asks.

"Dunno." Jon hands the envelope to her and tosses the rest of the mail on the hall table, loosening his tie.

As Liz opens the note, something drops out. Jon bends down to pick it up and realizes that it is a five-dollar gas card. "Huh . . . who is this from?" He leans in to scan the note over Liz's shoulder. "That's something else," he muses after a moment.

She hands him the note with a smile. "Seriously," she says, "I am impressed."

96-Hour Snail-Mail Response—The Handwritten Note

The 96-Hour Snail-Mail Response is something every church can do. By Thursday afternoon of the week they visited, you should have a personal, handwritten note in the hands of every person who provided you with a mailing address. If you are in an email-literate culture, this will follow the 36-Hour Email. If not, this is your post-weekend starting point.

The 96-Hour Snail-Mail Response consists of a handwritten note and a small, appropriate gift. You can also include a postcard from your current message series or some other piece of relevant information. We'll get to the logistics of getting this done in a minute, but first let's examine the details of this mailing's what and why.

Sending your guests a personalized, handwritten, first-class-stamped card is well worth the time and effort it requires. Lots of churches follow up by using a computer program that lets them input names and run off form letters, which are then stuffed into business-sized envelopes. People are used to getting letters like that in the mail—and they usually get tossed aside. I highly recommend taking personalization to the next level when dealing with first-time guests.

Think about it this way: When you go to your mailbox, what catches your eye first? Anything that is not shaped and formatted like a bill, right? And something that has your name handwritten on the front always makes it to the top of the pile. When your guests open their mailboxes on Thursday afternoon, do you want them getting a standard form letter from you that will wind up in the bill/unsolicited mail pile, or something that strikes them as special—something out of the ordinary that they'll want to open right away? A handwritten note goes a long way toward making your guests feel valued as individuals, rather than making them feel like they just got added to a list for more junk mail that they don't really want.

The 96-Hour Snail-Mail Response also gives you the perfect opportunity to wow your guests with another little surprise gift. Don't mention on Sunday that they'll be receiving something in the mail. Let it be a completely unexpected treat. At our Journey locations in Manhattan, we usually include a five-dollar subway MetroCard and write something along the lines of "Take a Journey on us!" in the note. We are essentially paying for their roundtrip return visit to the church. In more suburban areas, a five-dollar gas card is a great gift. Everyone appreciates a gesture that helps them fill a basic need. You can always do something a little more fun like a Starbucks card—many churches do—but in this first mailing, I recommend sticking with a gift that strikes a more basic nerve.

You may be thinking, *Great! I like the idea in theory, but how much is that going to cost me?* In working with and studying churches around the country, I have found that growing churches spend $400 to $500 on evangelism for each person who walks through the door as a first-time guest. Talk about an investment. If you've made it to the point of sending out this note to each guest, that investment has been worth it! Your guest showed up and left his or her contact information. But as the business world knows, it's always harder to get a return visit than an initial visit. So isn't it worth a free book at the service and another five dollars or so for a gift card to follow up with your guest in a way that will make him or her much more likely to come again? This is not an expense to your bottom line but an investment in keeping the unchurched people—the gifts—God sends your way.

In the sample note below, we include the MetroCard, a subway map, a business card from the pastor who taught on Sunday, and an information card about the current message series:

Hi [guest's name],

  Great to see you on Sunday at The Journey. We hope your time with us was both meaningful and relevant to your life—and that you had a good time, too!

Enclosed is a five-dollar MetroCard, good on all NYC subways and buses . . . so take a Journey on us! We hope to see you again soon. Hope you have a great week.

God bless,
[your name]
[your title, church name]
[your email address]

The handwritten note is really the keystone of the Fusion assimilation system. If you don't do anything else detailed in these pages, I challenge you to start sending a short, handwritten note to every first-time guest who visits your church. This one thing will revolutionize your assimilation efforts. Over and over, pastors who implement the Fusion system tell me that everything changed for them when they started sending handwritten notes.

While the handwritten note is powerful no matter where you are in the world, it resonates with people even more in cultures that have become extremely high tech, like ours. Why? A handwritten note is inherently high touch. It is a thoughtful, personal gesture in a world where so much of our lives are lived online, through social media, and on our phones. Receiving a special note in the mail will cause your guests to pay attention to you. Often, second-time guests will approach me after a service and say something like: "I got your note last week. You're the first person who has sent me anything handwritten since my birthday." I often hear about first-time guests posting a picture of the handwritten note they received to social media, commenting on how much it struck them. This simple touch carries more weight than you can imagine.

You may be thinking: *Sounds great, but I have five first-time guests every week. You mean I have to find the time to sit down and write five notes?* Yes, that's exactly what I mean. I know you're busy. You may think that you don't have time to handwrite notes for your first-timers—but in reality, the opposite is true. You don't have time not to. The handwritten note is so integral to the assimilation of your guests that it will influence the overall health and growth of your church. I would dare say that if you are not willing to do handwritten notes, then you are not in a position where God can trust you with more first-time guests.

When I teach at The Journey, I write thirty notes per week. Often, I try to get ahead by starting to write them midweek for the upcoming Sunday. The content of each note is pretty identical, so I can write the body and just leave off the name of the guest. After our services, all I have to do is go back to the notes and write *Hi* _____ and then address the envelope. If you walk into my office, you'll often see piles of notes that I've written during downtime, written while waiting for appointments, or written while sitting on airplanes. The time is there; you just have to identify it and seize it.

Only when we have more than thirty first-time guests at a service will I sometimes recruit other staff to help me write the notes. I encourage you to take the same approach. One of the big reasons I'm passionate about writing at least the first thirty notes myself is that this hands-on activity gives me a perfect opportunity to pray over our first-time guests. As I pen each card, I pray specifically for the person who will be receiving it. I pray that God will use it to touch each individual recipient and to draw him or her back for a second visit. When you hit the point of having others who help you write the notes, remind them to pray in the same way. As you take the time to reach out to your guests in this personal way and to pray over them in the process, God will do his part to bring them back to your church.

One-Month Follow-Up Letter

What if you have first-time guests who visit your church and you follow up in the ways we've discussed, but a month later they still haven't returned? There are a couple of things to keep in mind here: first of all, it's not unusual for unchurched people to visit a church and then stay away for a month or two before coming again. Just because you haven't heard from them doesn't mean they aren't coming back.

That being said, your focus should always be on securing return visits from last Sunday's first-time guests, not chasing down guests from months ago. You want everyone to return, but you don't want to expend undue energy on the unresponsive. Knowing how to walk this tightrope between reaching out and wasting time is difficult. At The Journey, we decided to do an additional personalized follow-up letter one month out via snail-mail and leave all future follow-up to our regular church mailings, our newsletter, and our special outreaches.

The purpose of the One-Month Follow-Up Letter is to remind your guests of their experience with your church, give them a little more information, and invite them back again. This is more of a form letter than your previous correspondence, but it still is not packaged in a business-sized envelope. At The Journey, we usually include a CD or DVD of a recent message—something relevant that will pique their interest. We are trying to make one last connection to secure a return visit.

Following up after a month is more important than you may think. So many first-time guests who don't return have simply fallen back into their normal Sunday routine. It's not that they are rejecting your initial follow-up—they are just putting off their return visit. When you make the effort to contact them a month later, not only do you remind them of their initial experience, but you also show them once more that they matter to you. It's a level of connection they are not expecting but will be glad to receive.

Every once in a while before a big event or a special service, we go back and pull the information for all of the unreturned first-time guests from the last year and send them an invitation. It's a great way to keep in touch even a little further out than one month. However, this is where your efforts to encourage unreturned first-time guests should end. Remember the golden rule when it comes to inviting people back after a certain amount of time: reach rather than reclaim. Growing churches put their energy into reaching new people that God is bringing their way, while stagnating churches focus on reclaiming people who have passed through and fallen away.

[Date]

Hi [first name],
It's hard to believe that it has been thirty days since your first visit!

We hope that you found The Journey to be a welcoming, relevant, and fun place to get plugged in and meet other people. We also hope you found The Journey to be a place where you could encounter God and have a meaningful worship experience.

To celebrate your one-month anniversary with The Journey, we have a gift that we hope helps you grow closer to God. It's a CD of a message we taught called "Getting Fit Spiritually." We pray you find it to be relevant to your own personal journey.

I also want to encourage you to get connected to a Growth Group this summer!

One of the best ways to meet new people and grow in your faith at The Journey is to sign up for a Growth Group.

Growth Groups are The Journey's groups of fifteen or so people who get together each week (Summer Growth Groups begin in June and last through August) in a convenient metro New York City location to grow and have fun together.

Sign-ups for our Summer Growth Groups have just started . . . and there are over sixty great groups to choose from. So . . . NOW is the perfect time to sign up!

You can sign up for a Summer Growth Group at any Journey service this Sunday or online TODAY at this link:

[web address]

Please let us know if there is any way that we can be praying for you. Have a wonderful week, and we look forward to seeing you again soon @ The Journey!

On the journey together . . .

[your signature]
[your title, church name]
[your email address]

P.S. Don't miss this Sunday as we begin our new teaching series, "Train to Win: Developing the Core Strengths of the Christian Faith," with the message "Personal God." See you there!

First Response Team

But you have a church to run, right? So how in the world can you be expected to do such extensive follow-up on your guests? As God blesses you with thirty or more first-time guests each week, you certainly can't do it all on your own, and your staff is stretched to the limit as it is, I know. That's where the First Response Team comes in.

The First Response Team is a group of volunteers who meet every Monday afternoon to help with all of the follow-up correspondence. Just let your members and regular attenders know they can swing by on Monday afternoons as they are free or on their way home from work to help you handwrite notes and take care of all the work that goes into following up with that week's guests. In the beginning, you and your staff may be able to handle it, but eventually as your evangelism outreach grows and God sends you more guests, don't hesitate to enlist the help of a few eager servers.

A strong First Response Team—one capable of handling all of the details—is crucial to the development of a dynamic follow-up strategy that will resonate with your first-time guests in a positive way.

Remember: everything speaks to your guests, and they don't stop listening when the service ends. While they may or may not be expecting correspondence from you, they will certainly be highly attuned to its timing (fast), heart (friendly), and relevance to their life (functionality) when they do receive something. If, on Sunday, you do a great job of *greeting*, *directing*, *treating*, and *seating* your guests in a powerful worship service and then succeed in getting their contact information, you will have climbed the steepest part of the mountain. You will have already created a positive, comfortable experience reflective of God's excellence and generosity.

But you can't stop there. Especially when dealing with the unchurched, you will increase your chances for a return visit tenfold when you reach into their weekly lives, genuinely thank them for joining you, and encourage them to come back by continuing to show them God's love in a practical, relevant way. It has been said: "In golf, as in life, it's the follow-through that counts." The same is true in your church. When it comes to keeping your guests, it's follow-up that counts. You've gotten them this far. You've built momentum. Don't stop midswing.

6

they're back!

We are what we repeatedly do. Excellence, then, is not an act, but a habit.

Aristotle

Let us consider how we may spur one another on toward love and good deeds.

Hebrews 10:24 NIV

I have several friends who like to bike in Central Park. The trees, the lake, the kids playing softball on lush green fields, and the smell of warm pretzels lingering on the breeze create an incomparable backdrop for a little exercise. The problem with biking in Central Park, however, is the hills. Though not monstrosities that would faze an experienced cyclist or even be a consideration to many semi-athletic mountain riders, they are pretty tough for Joe Average on his Huffy. While grunting up those hills, I'm told, the key is to focus on what's ahead—that impending, glorious shift in momentum when you crest the top and begin to coast down the backside of your effort, the exertion behind you suddenly worth every second as you relish the beauty of its reward.

I don't bike, but I can relate. That's exactly how I feel when guests walk back through The Journey's door for a second visit.

The Magic of Momentum

When your guests return for a second look, you've won 80 percent of the battle of gaining new regular attenders and have drastically increased the chances that they will begin a journey with Christ. The subtle momentum shift that occurs is priceless. Until this point, you've been putting in the hard work to win them as first-time guests, make them feel comfortable on their initial visit, get their contact information, wow them into seeing that there's something special going on at your church, and follow up with them in a way that entices them to come back. You've been screaming through your metaphorical megaphone, "Hey, look—we care about you! God cares about you! Come find out about his plan for your life!" You've been jumping up and down and waving your arms—internally, at least—while they've been sitting on the receiving end, guzzling up the benefits of your efforts.

When your guests hit the door for the second time, they are saying, "Okay, I'm interested. I want to find out more about this place. I want to find out more about God. Here I am again. Let's see where this goes." Many first-time guests are dragged to church by someone else or, as in Jon and Liz's case, attend to get someone off their back. When they decide to return for a second time, it's usually out of their own volition. Their interest has been piqued and they are making the effort to reengage. They are picking up their end of responsibility in the conversation you've started with them, or at least they're toying with picking it up. This shift is subtle but very real—and incredibly exciting for a pastor who wants nothing more than to see those guests reaching out a hand.

It's Saturday night. The kids are in bed. Jon and Liz sit on their back patio, reading. He's still wrapped up in *Unshakable*. She's finally making it to the day's newspaper.

"You want to meet up with Will and Jaime for brunch tomorrow?" Liz asks, pulling out the business section. "They left a message a little while ago."

Jon doesn't answer.

"Did you hear me?"

"Yeah," Jon says. "Could we do it late?"

"I guess. I'll talk to her in the morning. Why?"

"I was thinking we might go back to FCC tomorrow."

"Really? Did Sam talk you into going again?"

"No, he's out of town. I just . . . this book is interesting . . . and I've been thinking about a couple of things the pastor said last week," Jon says. "Did I tell you I used that gas card today?"

"No." Liz is hesitant but happy to hear Jon talking this way.

"What do you think?"

After a pause, Liz says, "I think it's a great idea. I'll tell Jaime we'll meet up with them later in the afternoon."

Jon turns back to his book. Liz gazes toward the sky. She's always wanted to have the kids in church, but no church ever seemed right—that's why they gave up on it years ago. And now Jon actually wants to go again. Could this be the place for them?

Ubiquity. If that's a word you are not familiar with, it's time to add it to your vocabulary. Defined as "presence everywhere at the same time," ubiquity is what you get when you have strong systems for assimilation in place. Think about it this way: If you have established a pre-service that allows you to effectively *greet, direct, treat,* and *seat* your first-time guests as they come through the door, won't you automatically be *greeting, directing, treating,* and *seating* your other attenders as well?

While the system may be geared specifically toward making your first-time guests feel welcomed and comfortable, it does the same for your second-time guests, your regular attenders, and your members by default. They all come through the same door. They are all greeted in the same way. They all get donuts and coffee. They are all ushered to a good seat. The system is ubiquitous—it exists everywhere on all levels of attendance at the same time.

With slight shifts of emphasis for the second-time guest, ubiquity works to your advantage for your during-service (Connection Card) and post-service (follow-up) strategies as well.

Communicating with Your Second-Time Guests

Once your second-timers have been *greeted*, *directed*, *treated*, and *seated* back into your service, what is your immediate goal for them? To, again, fill out the Connection Card. Thanks to the system's ubiquity, much of what we've already learned about the Connection Card translates directly from your first-time guests to your second-time guests, regular attenders, and members. You want everyone to fill out their contact information, check the box that indicates the status of their attendance, and take some personal Next Steps. That being said, your focus should narrow a bit when dealing with second-timers, as there are a couple of specific things you want to encourage them to do.

1. Encourage them to check the "Second-Time Guest" box.

Getting your second-time guest to fill out the Connection Card probably won't be too difficult, as they are expecting it. Still, in your announcement about the card, say something such as, "If you are a first- or second-time guest, let us know that by checking the appropriate box." Be sure to reiterate the importance of checking the correct box. You will benefit greatly from seeing how many second-time guests you have in your congregation. When you can see that people are returning for a second visit, you know your assimilation system is working. Such valuable information must be measured.

But even without your invitation, most of your second-timers will be eager to fill out the information and let you know that they are back for another look. Why? Because the last time they played along, they got a free gift in the mail. There's an undeniable principle that comes into play here: *That which gets rewarded gets repeated.* By getting it right with them on their first visit and by rewarding them in an unexpected way during the week, you are going to see a much higher percentage of second-time guests showing up and letting you know they've shown up. Even if part of their motivation at this point is the hope of another free gift, that's okay. You are moving them through a process.

2. Encourage deeper involvement through a Next Step.

In addition to letting you know they're there, you want your return guests to indicate a Next Step on the back of the Connection Card—specifically, a Next Step that will get them involved in some way. Now that they're back, your main objective is to help them connect on a deeper level. As we discussed, taking a Next Step calls your guests to action and gives them a sense of commitment.

As we saw in chapter 4, Next Steps are important for your first-timers, too. Many, like Liz, will be comfortable enough to check a few during that first visit. But the steps your first-time guests choose are generally noncommittal, such as a request for more information or an agreement to memorize the verse of the week. Your goal with the second-timers is to encourage them to take a Next Step that will get them involved in a serving opportunity, connect them with a small group, or make them want to attend a special event—anything that nudges them along the continuum to a point of deeper involvement. Make sure you follow up on each Next Step as appropriate for your church's culture.

Pointed repetition usually spurs people to action. Your second-time guests will be much more likely to identify a Next Step that requires a higher level of commitment if you give them several opportunities. At The Journey, we introduce Next Steps for the first time about twenty minutes into the service. We do not want to introduce the Connection Card too early, to be sure not to miss the late arrivers. Again, as we welcome everyone and encourage them to fill out the information on the front of the Connection Card, we'll also say something along the lines of, "If you flip your Connection Card over to the back, you'll notice several Next Steps you can take today. We'll be referring to these steps throughout the service, so keep your card close by." Then during the message, we make a point of repeatedly drawing their attention back to the card.

For example, if I am in the middle of a message point on the importance of having other believers in your life, I may say, "Look at the back of your card. If you know that you need to have other believers in your life, one of the ways you can do that is by taking the Next Step to attend our coffeehouse this Friday night, where you can meet some other believers." There will be an appropriate box for them to check, saying that they would like to attend the coffeehouse. The key is to give each second-timer an opportunity for action at the moment he or she is thinking: *You know, he's right. I do need more believers in my life*, or whatever the specific case may be. If your second-timers are ready to respond, you don't want to stall that reaction by waiting until the end of your sermon to call for a decision. When your people are ready to take action, extend the invitation and let them act.

You can also use the same technique to encourage second-timers to sign up for a service opportunity, join a small group, or get more information about Membership Class. Then, of course, you bring up the card again at the very end of the service, encourage them once more to take the Next Step that is right for them, and ask them to drop the card in the offering bucket as it is passed. Ubiquitously, this call to action entices everyone from first-time guests to long-time members to take a Next Step.

The back of the Connection Card is your guests' single point of response to your message. It negates the need for sign-up sheets in the church lobby and other similar mechanisms. In working with countless churches, we have found that keeping the communication centralized to one place—the card—is the most effective way of encouraging people to indicate their interest and the best way to simplify communication for you.

On the back of our Connection Card, the Next Steps on the right-hand side of the card are standard—these are the options that remain the same week to week. The Next Steps on the left-hand side are customized weekly, based on the message content and on church events. Keeping the card alive through customization adds to the sense of urgency around each decision. In the customized portion, we always try to have at least three action steps that relate to the topic of the message and one that encourages an assimilation step. If your church is not at a point of being able to customize weekly, just make sure that you have a wide range of response options available on your card until you are.

The ubiquitous nature of the Connection Card allows it to serve all of your communication needs for all of your attenders. It is a tool that will be universally accepted and utilized once integrated into your church culture. (Again, the process of ingraining the card into your church's collective consciousness usually takes about six months.) While the emphasis and use of the card will shift as your attenders move through the assimilation process, its presence gives each and every individual sitting in your congregation an opportunity to respond to the message in a tangible way—an act of engagement that is important for everyone but absolutely essential for encouraging your second-timers to take that step of deeper involvement.

Following Up with Your Second-Time Guests

Let's keep coasting down this hill, shall we? When it comes to following up with your second-time guests, the process looks very much like it did with the first-timers.

36-Hour Second-Time Email Response

Follow-up starts with another 36-Hour Email Response. You want to accomplish three things with this email, two of which parallel what you did in the first-time email and one that goes a step further:

1. Thank your guests for returning.
2. Invite them to fill out the second-time guest survey.
3. Give them more opportunities to get plugged in and include a link that will help them take a Next Step (this is the new part).

117

Subject: Glad to have you back at The Journey!

From: [Your name (or name of the pastor who taught on Sunday, if not you)]

Hi [guest's name],

I'm glad that you were able to join us again Sunday at The Journey. It's good to know that we did not scare you off after your first time with us :-). I hope you enjoyed your second time as we talked about "Friendship: Wireless Connections."

There are a lot of easy ways to get plugged in at The Journey. If you have not already, you can sign up for the Growth Group of your choice on any Sunday or during the week anytime on our website [link]. I hope you decide to get plugged into one of our small groups.

We would love for you to take thirty seconds to fill out one more survey for us. Just click here or visit our website [link] and let us know how you felt about your second visit to The Journey. We want to know your thoughts so that we can serve you better.

I will be praying for you this week. If there is anything specific that we can be praying for you about, if you have any questions, or if there is anything we can do for you this week, please don't hesitate to let me know.

Have a great week and God bless,

[your name]
[your title, church name]

P.S. Don't forget: This weekend we continue our series "Life 360" at The Journey. You don't want to miss it! Invite a friend, too. I look forward to seeing you then.

For example, if the second visit falls during a small group sign-up period, include a link to your website that provides more information about groups and prompts them to sign up online. If you want to encourage them to connect through volunteering, mention it in the email and link to a page with more information. You're looking for anything that will get them to take a step toward involvement. As we'll see in the next chapter, getting your second-time guests involved in situations where they can connect with others is the key to making them stick.

The information we get from the second-time guest surveys is always more powerful than what we get from the first-timers. If someone has visited for a second time and is now willing to fill out another survey, they are starting to pull for you. They want to help. They want you to know what they think of the church. They want to express their opinion and tell you if they would bring friends with them. Their candid reactions are an extremely helpful tool. While we don't want actual critiques from our first-time guests, we do from the second-time guests. We've found that second-timers give feedback in a way that helps to draw them in rather than pushing them away.

96-Hour Second-Time Snail-Mail Response

As with first-time follow-up, make sure your second-time guests receive a letter in the mail no later than Thursday after the Sunday of their second visit. This time around, we don't send a handwritten note. Instead, we send a typed letter (still no business envelope, though!) that thanks them for coming back and gives them more information about how they can get involved. Let your second-timer know you understand the significance of their decision to come back, and tell them how they can take steps toward deeper spiritual commitment and community involvement.

The letter's content is similar to the email they will have just received. If it's Growth Group season, we promote groups. If not, we promote a fun event or special service that's coming up soon. (For a downloadable version of this and all other guest letters, visit www.FusionBook.com.)

[Date]

Hi [First name],

It was great to see you again at The Journey on Sunday. We're excited that you chose to check out The Journey a second time! To show our appreciation, we have enclosed a Starbucks card for a free beverage on us. We hope you enjoy it.

I also want to encourage you to get connected to a Growth Group this summer!

One of the best ways to meet new people and grow in your faith at The Journey is to sign up for a Growth Group. Growth Groups are The Journey's groups of fifteen or so people who get together each week (Summer Growth Groups begin in June and last through August) in a convenient Metro New York City location to grow and have fun together.

Sign-ups for our Summer Growth Groups have just started . . . and there are over sixty great groups to choose from. So . . . NOW is the perfect time to sign up!

You can sign up for a Summer Growth Group at any Journey service this Sunday or online TODAY at this link:

[web address]

Please let us know if there is anything we can do for you or if there is a specific way that we can be praying for you this week.

We look forward to seeing you this Sunday. Have a great week, and God bless!

On the journey . . .

> *[your signature]*
> *[your name]*
> *[your title, church name]*
> *[your email address]*

P.S. Don't forget: This weekend we continue "Life 360" by examining how we can have a high-definition faith. You will not want to miss it! Invite a friend to come with you. We look forward to seeing you then.

So as not to let the wow factor fall, we also include a small gift in this follow-up letter. Remember the principle that encouraged your second-time guests to fill out their Connection Card and check the boxes? *That which gets rewarded gets repeated.* You've established an expectation and don't want to disappoint. By enclosing another little gift—something more fun this time, like a Starbucks card or a gift card for a local frozen yogurt shop—you are solidifying for them that, yes, you really do care. They've come back a second time, and you are still reaching out with love. They see that your surprising service to them was not just a gimmick, that you still want to bless them in some small way.

For all you number crunchers, don't worry. This is the last gift card you'll be sending in the mail. But at this crucial juncture, it is more than worth your while to meet and exceed your second-time guests' expectations so that they'll continue the process toward becoming regular attenders.

Ubiquity and Omnipresence

God's omnipresence allows him to be in all places at the same time—to be universally present. Ubiquity, in the way we've been exploring it, is our effort to bring a similar overarching presence to the systems of his church. Ubiquity works in favor of your assimilation system once you've set up a solid mechanism for your pre-service, Connection Cards, and follow-up. The momentum you gain in getting everything right for first-time guests pays big dividends as you start seeing the reward of that labor with your second-timers and regular attenders.

Think of the alternative: How can we possibly help people understand the power of an omnipotent God if we, as a church, are hit or miss from week to week? If we are scrambling to do one thing for one group of attenders and something different for the next? If we are catering to one set of people at the expense of another? Having systems in place that are ubiquitous by their very nature allows us to welcome and encourage all of our attenders equally. In doing so, we reflect the order and consistent excellence that God demands. As Aristotle said, "We are what we repeatedly do. Excellence, then, is not an act, but a habit."

In the case of a strong assimilation system, excellence truly is the result of an established habit—a ubiquitous system—that allows us to touch and influence first-timers, second-timers, regular attenders, and members effectively week after week. Through such a system, your attenders will be rewarded and their attendance will be repeated, allowing them more opportunities to discover the true meaning of excellence in their own lives.

7

sticky situations

Friendship is born at that moment when one person says to another: "What! You too? I thought I was the only one."

C. S. Lewis

It is not good for the man to be alone. I will make a helper who is just right for him.

God (Gen. 2:18)

This Sunday, churches across America will be filled with transient attenders, those churchgoers who come in a few minutes late, head straight to their seats, participate in worship, listen attentively to the message, and duck out without talking to anyone when the service is over. Though their behavior is similar to that of first-time or second-time guests, they are not. They are relatively new regular attenders who want to be involved in the church but who don't know how to step out and form relationships with others around them.

You may be thinking: *Well, at least they are there. They come. They may even give. How much can we expect? Sure, it would be good for them to develop godly relationships, but that's not as important as what they are learning through the message. Relationships will happen in time, right?* Wrong. If these well-intentioned people don't connect with someone soon, they will disappear in four to six months.

Two Roads Diverged in a Second-Time Guest's Life

When your second-time guests walk through your door, they unknowingly come face-to-face with a fork in the road. Four to six months from that moment, they will either be assimilated into your church or they will be gone—far from the church and likely far from any kind of relationship with Jesus. Your job is to guide them in the right direction with the opportunities and encouragement that are essential to their journey while you have the chance. Let's look at where each of these two diverging roads leads.

Road One—If you take the time and effort to guide them down Road One, your second-timers will be introduced to comfortable, hospitable environments where they can meet and connect with other people. They will form relationships that will give them a sense of belonging. Within a few weeks, they will know that people care about them, and they will care about others in return. The young friendships you have helped them establish will keep them on the path toward becoming followers of Jesus, dedicated regular attenders and, eventually, members.

Road Two—Road Two is, sadly, the road second-timers in most American churches end up taking. Too many churches fail to recognize the importance of plugging in second-time guests and new attenders. Left on their own, with little insight on how to connect at a deeper level, newcomers will meander the path of least resistance. Sure, they may be asked to sign up for a potluck in the fellowship hall or join one of the church's small groups (a group that has probably been together for months or even years), but being uncomfortable with most of the opportunities and the way those opportunities are presented, they will be pushed further down Road Two. Unfortunately, Road Two leads to the church abyss. These travelers will move from being new attenders to transient attenders—that is, until they leave the church altogether.

Imagine the lonesome, uncomfortable feeling of the new church attenders who see groups of friends talking, laughing, heading to lunch after the service week after week, yet they have no one to talk to and aren't sure how to reach out. Those feelings will make it increasingly difficult to return with each passing week. Especially if they don't yet have a relationship with Jesus, the sheer social dynamics and pressure of being lone rangers will eventually start to keep them away.

You have ninety days to get people connected. In my experience studying trends, measuring our research at The Journey, and working with other churches around the country, I have found that the more friends people have by the ninety-day mark, the more likely they are to stay. If, after ninety days, they are still wandering through services disconnected, then they are significantly more likely to drop off the radar.

Makes sense, doesn't it? Our need for human connection is undeniable. God formed us for relationships with the words, "It is not good for the man to be alone."

Of course, some relationships will happen on their own—but if you and I want to lead growing churches filled with fully developing followers of Jesus, we can't count on that. We can't leave relational connections to happenstance. We have to proactively help people form healthy friendships. As assimilators, it is up to us to shine the light down the path toward relationships, not down the path of least resistance. If we do our job well, each of our newcomers will be able to echo the words of Robert Frost: "I took the road less traveled by, and that has made all the difference."

Creating Stickiness

Relationships are the glue that will cause your second-timers to stick. Connections with the body of Christ are the most effective adhesive for keeping your guests and your church bound together. So how can you help your second-time guests form these important connections? By getting them involved in sticky situations.

We have discovered four effective engagement opportunities that give people the best possible chance to be comfortable getting involved: small groups, fun events, service teams, and newcomer receptions.

1. Small Groups

The Sunday service is your front door. It's where people are introduced to your church for the first time. What you don't want is for people to walk through the front door, stay a while, and then head out through the back. Small groups are the single best way to close that back door. Research shows that once someone gets involved in a small group, that person is much more likely to stay in church. Why? Because he or she will know people and be known to them. Relationships with other spiritual-growth-minded people will be formed. The church and the small group will be thought of as a type of family—as a home.

The Journey's small group system—often referred to as the Activate system—is a little different from what you may be used to. While we have respect for the Sunday school model of small groups and see its value for many churches, we have chosen a decentralized system with the goal of involving all of our regular adult attenders. Our small groups generally yield 100 percent church participation. That means we keep close to 100 percent of the new attenders who choose to get involved in a group.

> **Four Sticky Situations**
>
> Small groups
> Fun events
> Service teams
> Newcomer receptions

Given the power of those numbers, we don't take small group participation lightly. We know that if we want someone to stick around long enough to discover the truth about Christ and experience true life change, we need to do all we can to encourage that person to sign up for a group.

Obviously we can't go into our entire small group process here. For a detailed study of the system, see my book *Activate: An Entirely New Approach to Small Groups*. But I do want to take this opportunity to hit on one of the key characteristics that encourages newcomer involvement: our small groups run in three three-month cycles, with a few weeks in between each cycle as a rest/sign-up period. In other words, we run a semester-based system—and we do so for some very compelling reasons.

The cold hard truth is that no matter how many wonderful small groups you have in place at your church, your new people do not want to join a show already in progress. Newcomers are always reluctant to jump into an intimate environment with a group of strangers who already know each other. They are much more comfortable getting involved in a group on the front end so that they don't feel as if they are breaking into an established circle. Your best efforts and intentions to encourage them otherwise cannot stand against this undeniable social-psychological fact. You can sell the openness and benefits of your current small groups until you are blue, but getting new people to join them will always be an uphill battle, and it's a battle you don't need to fight.

Goethe said, "That which matters most must never be at the mercy of that which matters least." At The Journey, we decided to work with our people instead of trying to pressure them into a traditional small group system that wasn't effectively serving their needs. Remember, people need to make some friends within about ninety days or they will not stick. That reality, combined with the fact that small groups are the best sticking opportunity, factored into our decision to create a new type of small group process—a semester-based system. No matter what time of year a new person begins attending our church—even if they miss the start of new groups by just a few weeks—there will always be a new cycle of groups waiting for them just over the horizon.

Semester-based small groups have many other advantages, as well. Leaders don't get burned out; regular attenders are continually connecting with more and more people within the church; busy people are more likely to commit because they know it's only for a certain period of time. I could go on and on, but that is another discussion for another time. (To learn all about creating a successful small group system, make sure to check out *Activate: An Entirely New Approach to Small Groups*.)

The point is that when it comes to assimilating your guests, your job is to create opportunities and environments that will serve them. Setting up your small groups in a way that most effectively encourages newcomer participation will help your new attenders form solid relationships with other believers, thus keeping them on the road to becoming fully developing followers of Jesus. (For audio teaching and additional resources on creating effective small groups, visit www.FusionBook.com.)

Jon and Liz's second visit to FCC looked a lot like their first. Only this time they were a little more comfortable because they knew their way around and had a sense of how the service worked. But they still hadn't really talked to anyone. Liz requested more information on small groups, which Jon thought a little premature, but he didn't say anything. During the service, Tim mentioned a picnic in the park scheduled for the following Saturday—a chance to relax and meet others in the church. Liz requested more information on that, too.

When the follow-up letter came on Thursday, it included a flyer outlining the picnic details. Jon stuck the flyer on the front of the refrigerator.

As Saturday morning rolls around, Jon wakes up thinking about going to the FCC picnic. Pouring himself a cup of coffee, he pulls the flyer off of the fridge and sits down at the kitchen table with Liz.

"What do you think about this?" he asks.

"We should go. Why not? The kids want to."

"Yeah, but we won't know anybody," Jon protests, playing his own nemesis.

"And we still won't know anybody if we don't go. That's the point. We need to really check out some of the other people at FCC—outside of church," says Liz.

"You know I hate making conversation with strangers."

"So we'll do our own thing and see if the chance to talk to someone opens up. It's not like we are going to go around interviewing everybody."

Jon sighs. He knows she's right. And he has been looking forward to the picnic in a strange way, but new situations are hard for him. Of course, if their experiences in the FCC services were any indication, this should be okay—maybe even fun.

"Well, it does say here that there'll be pickup football. It wouldn't hurt me to teach some Christian guys a few moves," Jon says with a wink.

Liz rolls her eyes. "Good. I'll pull the picnic basket out of the attic."

---

2. Fun Events

Fun events give people the chance to get to know each other in a more social environment, which leads to deeper connections and relationships. These events can be anything from a Saturday picnic in the park to a bowling night, a paintball game to a pottery class. The possibilities are endless. You can also organize fun events around a message series you are planning to teach. For instance, when we are teaching our annual God on Film series, we schedule weekly events to go see and discuss the upcoming film in the series. You can also piggyback on local happenings. If your city is hosting a big summer or fall festival, make it a fun event for your church. Invite everyone to meet up and go together.

Fun events are a perfect opportunity for your second-time guests to get involved for three reasons: They are (1) low-pressure, (2) low-commitment, and, well, (3) lots of fun! Because these events, by their very nature, draw different people every time, your second-time guests will be more likely to attend. They know that this will be a casual, one-time gathering, likely filled with people who don't already know each other that well. And being one-time excursions, these fun events require a lower level of commitment from your guests than just about anything else they can attend. The best thing about fun events, though, is that they are enjoyable activities that newcomers truly want to be involved in. Your guests will probably be intrigued that the church is inviting them to have a good time. Depending on their backgrounds, they will be excited to see how people who love and honor Jesus can live the fun parts of life together, too.

Planning your fun events strategically will pay off. In general, churches see their number of guests increase early in the year and then again in the fall. Keep that in mind when you are planning your fun events for the year. If you have a lot of second-time guests and new attenders in February, plan more events than usual in March. Give your guests as many opportunities as possible to say yes to connecting with others.

Also, as mentioned, be strategic in planning some fun events around activities your guests will be taking part in anyway. For example, in Manhattan, movies are a part of life, a fact we take advantage of consistently. When a new blockbuster comes out, most people in our demographic are planning to see it. So if we can encourage our guests and new attenders to see the film with a group of like-minded people from the church and then go to dinner after to talk about it, we are only asking them to do something they would be doing anyway. They may not even be thinking about forming connections and making new friends through the process, and they don't have to. Because of our efforts to structure and facilitate the opportunity, relationships start to happen naturally.

3. Service Teams

Another engagement opportunity we offer second-time guests is the chance to get involved with our service teams. We believe there are many areas of service that can be open to those who don't yet have a relationship with Christ, such as helping with the refreshments table or ushering people to their seats. If guests have been impressed with their initial experiences within your church, many of them will be interested in offering that service back to others. Giving them the opportunity to engage in service moves them further along the continuum of the assimilation process.

God can use your newcomers to serve others even if they don't personally know him yet. It's not like they are going to be counseling people. They will be smiling and handing out programs or directing people to the children's area. Cutting them off from this opportunity based on their current level of spiritual maturity could slow down or negatively impact their progression. Encouraging an unbeliever to serve in no way hinders you, and it could mean the world to the unbeliever. We've found that allowing non-Christians to rub shoulders with Christians and see the church in action can be very beneficial in their journey toward Christ, as we will explore further in chapter 8.

Service teams are particularly good at helping people stick to your church for several reasons. As with small groups and fun events, service teams provide an ideal opportunity for your second-time guests to form relationships with other people in the church. But serving also accomplishes some things above and beyond the critical friendship factor. It makes people feel alive. Serving is invigorating and incredibly rewarding. Plus, when you give your second-time guests the opportunity to serve, they will begin to see your church in a different light. They will see themselves as givers rather than takers, which will lead to a sense of ownership. As we will see in the next chapter, that sense of ownership and the accompanying sense of responsibility leads them to the point of wanting to become members. (For more on creating environments where people love to serve, see my book *Connect: How to Double Your Number of Volunteers*. Also visit www.FusionBook.com for additional serving resources.)

4. Newcomer Receptions

Hosting newcomer receptions is a great way for you to meet and talk with the new people God is bringing you. I suggest planning several Sunday afternoon newcomer receptions throughout the year, strategically scheduled one to two weeks after you've had a Big Day in your church—for example, after the kickoff of a new series, Easter, or any other Sunday that would likely bring a high number of guests. (For more on the importance of Big Days, see my book *Ignite: How to Spark Immediate Growth in Your Church*.) These newcomer receptions will draw second-time guests plus all of those who have already turned into new regular attenders.

Getting your newcomers to a reception is key to creating early relationships. Not only does the reception give you the chance to meet your new people, it also gives them the chance to meet you and other staff members at your church. This is a critically important aspect of creating stickiness. When new attenders have had an opportunity to talk with the pastor and other leaders personally, they will feel more valued and more engaged with the church as a result. Plus, the newcomer reception allows those new to your church to meet and mingle with others who are at a similar point on the journey toward becoming fully engaged members.

In the midst of this socializing and relationship building, you will be able to use your newcomer reception to help new attendees start becoming connected to the life of your church. This is your chance to talk with them about the importance of getting involved in a small group, joining in on an upcoming fun event, and serving at the weekend service. You can also plant early seeds for baptism and membership. When your second-time guests and new regular attenders leave a well-facilitated newcomer reception, they will have made a couple of new friends and already be planning to join in on another sticky situation soon. (For more on promoting and hosting an effective newcomer reception, visit www .FusionBook.com.)

Not for Friends' Sake

God created people to live in relationship, but in the process of assimilation, we are not encouraging our second-timers to make friends merely for the sake of having more friends. Rather, we understand that connecting them with people in the church is a biblical command. We are integrating them into the body so that they can continue to grow toward knowing Jesus Christ. In *How People Grow: What the Bible Reveals about Personal Growth*, Dr. Henry Cloud and Dr. John Townsend write:

> People's most basic need in life is relationship. . . . Ironically, one problem we often see in the Christian community is that people get more into religion and less into the connectedness the Bible prescribes. . . . Many people feel disconnected from God because they have not been connected to his Body. Paul describes the problem this way: "He has lost connection with the Head, from whom the whole body, supported and held together by its ligaments and sinews, grows as God causes it to grow" (Col. 2:19). The clear teaching of the New Testament is that the Body of Christ is to be people deeply connected to each other.[1]

By inviting people into relationship with others in the church, we are taking the next step in giving them the best possible opportunity to become fully developing followers of Christ. The alternative—the other road—leads only to frustration and disillusionment with the church and likely with God himself. As Jesus said:

> "You must love the Lord your God with all your heart, all your soul, and all your mind." This is the first and greatest commandment. A second is *equally* important: "Love your neighbor as yourself." The entire law and all the demands of the prophets are based on these two commandments. (Matt. 22:37–40, emphasis added)

Helping your second-time guests learn to love their neighbors is, according to Jesus, equally as important as learning to love God. And for your assimilation process, giving second-time guests opportunities to do the former will help open the door for them to do the latter.

8

taking ownership

Action springs not from thought, but from a readiness for responsibility.

G. M. Trevelyan

And let us not neglect our meeting together, as some people do, but encourage one another, especially now that the day of his return is drawing near.

Hebrews 10:25

Jon and Liz made it through the picnic unscathed. In fact, they enjoyed themselves. They connected with some other couples who live close by, and the kids made a couple of friends. Jon even exchanged phone numbers with one of the guys in the pickup football game and tentatively scheduled a time to grab coffee.

A couple Sundays later, Jon finds himself ushering people to their seats after Liz greets them at the door. He's not sure how he got signed up for this, but he doesn't really mind. Being on the serving end of things actually excites him in a strange way. He finds himself wanting to make sure that everyone who walks in the door of FCC has a good experience. He feels a responsibility to do his job well because he was so pleasantly surprised by the people in this role when he first visited. What was that, six weeks ago now? Time flies.

The Role of Responsibility

Responsibility and ownership go hand in hand. When we are given responsibility in the workplace, within our families, or in a social environment, we naturally feel a sense of ownership over what we are responsible for. Think about jobs you've had in the past. When your boss appointed you responsible for a project, it automatically became your project, didn't it? Your responsibility to guide the project made you its owner.

On the other side of that coin, when we take ownership over something ourselves, we naturally feel an accompanying sense of responsibility toward it. Remember your first car? I bet you took incredible care to wash it, check the oil, and keep the gas tank full. Your ownership of that vehicle put you in charge of its best interests. Ownership and responsibility are inseparable. They are as interconnected and as dependent on each other as Chinese philosophy's yin and yang.

The interdependent nature of responsibility and ownership works in favor of your assimilation system. When your regular attenders begin taking on responsibility, they will start to feel a real sense of ownership. As your church becomes their church, they will reach toward membership as their natural next step. In this case, responsibility precedes ownership, and ownership precedes membership. We'll examine the mental shift that occurs in more detail momentarily, but first let's take a look at how this idea of responsibility builds on where we've come from.

THE THREE *R*'s OF RETENTION

Return   Relationships   Responsibility

In its simplest form, the tenets of the entire Fusion assimilation system can be boiled down to the three *R*'s of retention: *return, relationships*, and *responsibility*. When those first-time guests walked through your door, your initial goal was to earn return visits from them. When they returned, your goal evolved. You wanted to introduce them to environments and situations that would encourage them to build relationships. As they moved from first-timers to second-timers and new regular attenders, your thinking shifted from *return* to *relationships*.

> *Responsibility will be the catalyst that moves people from regular attendance to membership.*

Now that they have made some friends and have become true regular attenders, your thinking needs to shift once again—this time from *relationships* to *responsibility*. Responsibility will be the catalyst that moves them from regular attendance to membership, which is the next and final level of the assimilation process. It doesn't matter how well you preach or how passionate your worship team is—if your newcomers do not find relationships and take on responsibility within the church, they will not stay long.

Return. Relationships. Responsibility. Make these three buzzwords your assimilation mantra.

Two Sundays later, Jon has just led a young couple, obviously first-timers, to their seats when he spots one of his co-workers, Anthony, coming through the door. About a month ago, Jon had heard Sam inviting Anthony to church. Jon had steered clear of the conversation, not yet sure how much he wanted to connect himself with FCC. But a lot has changed over the last month, and now he's glad to see that Anthony has decided to visit. As Anthony makes his way toward the aisle, Jon waves.

"Hey, man," says Jon, shaking Anthony's hand. "Good to see you here. Did Sam invite you?"

"Yeah," says Anthony, glancing around. "I figured I would have to show up at least once to get him off my back." Anthony chuckles and then looks at Jon with renewed interest. "You go to this church?"

"Yep. This is our church. We've been here for a couple of months now. It's a great place. I'm glad you came."

"Wow. Okay. I . . . I didn't know that," Anthony stammers.

"Here. Let me grab you a seat. The service is about to start. I'll catch up with you after."

"Uh, okay. Thanks, Jon," Anthony says, as he follows Jon down the aisle.

Making the Mental Shift

The sense of ownership that accompanies responsibility manifests itself in your attenders' language. Attenders who have not moved into the realm of ownership will inevitably refer to the church as *your church* when talking to you or other attenders. In telling their friends about the church, they may call it *that church*.

Once they begin to sense ownership, however, their language changes. *Your church* becomes *our church* and conversations with others make mention of *my church*. These linguistic subtleties are a good gauge of where people are on the assimilation continuum. A sense of ownership will always precede interest in membership, so it is vital for you to help your attenders make the mental shift. And what breeds that sense of ownership? Responsibility.

As long as they are not taking on responsibility, your attenders will approach church with a consumer mentality. They may not even realize it, but you have to stay aware. The attenders who make a weekly habit of coming in, sitting through the worship service, and then leaving it all behind until the next Sunday will quickly fall into a dangerous, selfish, *what is the church doing for me?* mind-set. They are takers, and all takers get spoiled. Only when they have a responsibility in seeing others exposed to the Good News will they understand the church from its proper perspective. Only then will they be engaging in the body the way that God intended. And only then will they truly begin to feel like the church is *their* church. This is when they will be ready to take the step of membership.

The four most effective ways to encourage your attenders toward membership work together with incredible synergy:

1. Encourage membership through multiplying service opportunities.
2. Encourage membership through teaching.
3. Encourage membership through regular sign-ups.
4. Encourage membership through small groups.

Let's look at each one in more detail.

1. Encourage membership through multiplying service opportunities.

You can never have enough people serving. Are you beginning to understand why? Of course you need volunteers to make your service run smoothly, but that's not the biggest reason you need people connected in service. Serving is more important to the spiritual growth of your attenders than it is to the success of your service. As your volunteers serve you and the church, you are serving them by providing them with an opportunity to take on responsibility and become more deeply connected. Given this truth, one of the best ways to encourage membership is to multiply your service opportunities. Provide your regular attenders with more ways to serve more often. Never let a lack of opportunity stand in the way of someone who wants to get involved. (For a detailed study on creating a strong volunteer system in your church that will allow you to connect more people through service, see my book *Connect: How to Double Your Number of Volunteers*.)

Many growing churches across the country are moving to a multiple service format. At The Journey, we currently have several identical services every Sunday in Manhattan and additional services around the metro area—that means multiple opportunities for our congregants to attend church and multiple services through which we can provide service opportunities. One of the best things about having several services is that they allow more people to become involved in greeting, ushering, manning refreshments, working with children, and so on. Your need for volunteers is multiplied as you multiply your services. What an opportunity for your regular attenders.

Obviously, I am in no way suggesting that you move to a multiservice format just so more people can volunteer, but if you already hold multiple services (or if you're ready to take that step), make sure you are using them to provide as many service opportunities for as many different regular attenders as possible. Never try to do more with fewer people. Rather, always be thinking about how you can do more with more people. I would have an usher for every row if that many people were willing to serve. (Visit www .FusionBook.com for information on when and how to start additional services.)

In working with many regular attenders who are not yet believers, we always face the question of how spiritual maturity factors into different areas of service. If an attender is not yet a believer, can that person serve in any area, or are there restrictions on service? At The Journey, we use the Ladder Principle to help us address this issue.

Think of your serving opportunities as a ladder, with each ascending rung of the ladder representing a higher level of service. Your regular attenders need to begin climbing the rungs of this ladder while they are still unbelievers. The climb itself helps them move toward a deeper knowledge of God. However, at a certain point on the ladder, the rungs become only accessible to those who are already believers.

For example, we don't allow regular attenders who are not yet believers to count the offering. They can collect the offering as ushers (a lower rung on the ladder), but they cannot be responsible for counting it. Unbelievers can play instruments in the background of the worship team, but they can't sing solos. Deciding where the service climb ends for your unbelievers or nonmembers is something you will have to seek God's wisdom on. Comfort levels are different for every church. Just be careful not to set the bar too low when dealing with your attenders who aren't yet Christians. Give them ample opportunities to become involved, take on responsibilities, and thrive in a service environment. These opportunities will contribute to their continued spiritual growth. Allow people to belong before they believe. (For a detailed examination of the Ladder Principle, see *Connect: How to Double Your Number of Volunteers*.)

2. Encourage membership through teaching.

Most of the unchurched first-time guests who go on to become your regular attenders have no base of knowledge concerning church membership. Even if they were raised in a church, they probably don't understand what it means to be part of the family of God, biblically speaking. It's not that people are against joining—people join things all the time and make big commitments to maintain their memberships. But with church membership, they simply don't know what they don't know, and you have a responsibility to educate them. There are two ways you can teach about membership and related issues, such as baptism, that will inform your regular attenders and move them to action.

First, try setting aside specific Sundays throughout the year to teach on the importance of church membership. In a simple and straightforward way, you can build an entire message around illustrating what it means to join with the body of Christ through membership. Talk to your congregation candidly about following Christ's example through baptism. Give them a biblical lesson on what it means to be a member of a thriving church. This will be eye-opening for the majority of your regular attenders—if they had understood the importance of membership, they would have already taken that step! The uninformed new believers who sit in your rows need to know that without being linked to the body, they are spiritual orphans. When they internalize this truth, they will want to pursue membership. For those who aren't yet believers, learning the biblical importance of membership may lead to an acknowledgment of their need for a Father. (For free transcripts of sermons on membership, go to www.FusionBook.com.)

Second, be on the lookout for opportunities to present membership as an answer to the problems your people are facing. For example, if you are preaching on overcoming loneliness or on forming biblical relationships, you have an open door to introduce and explain the importance of being a part of the family of God. Your regular attenders have needs that can be met only by entering into a relationship with Christ and becoming part of his church. They may sense that need as a feeling of loneliness or a yearning to belong. When you address their feelings and then give them the good news that they have a spiritual family waiting for them with open arms, the message resonates in a powerful way. They see their relational needs in light of God's grace, and they want to take the steps toward becoming who they were meant to be in him.

As your regular attenders begin to take ownership in your church, they will only become frustrated if they don't understand the facts of membership and continued growth. You cannot neglect your role in making sure they have the knowledge to support their development. In all likelihood, your new attenders are ignorant about the things of God. They lack understanding and training. As you have walked them through the assimilation process, they have been learning things about God's goodness and his people. Hopefully they have come to a point of accepting him into their lives. However, they will still be ignorant and disconnected if you don't teach them what it means to be a member and then provide them with a simple opportunity to take that step.

3. Encourage membership through regular sign-ups.

Once your regular attenders decide they want to be members, how do they go about joining? How clear is the process? In discussing this aspect of assimilation with churches across the country, I have found that a surprisingly large majority have no clear-cut system for helping people take the step of membership. They simply expect a prospective member to call the church office, talk to the pastor, or stop by the resource table. They rarely outline a specific way for someone to express interest in membership. Such a lack of clarity keeps a lot of people from joining. Then there are the churches that require a prospective member to fill out a membership form that would intimidate—and maybe even disqualify—Billy Graham. This, too, keeps prospective members at a distance.

To encourage tentative regular attenders to pursue membership, make the process as clear and simple as possible. People don't like to sign on for anything when they don't fully understand how to go about it. They will also steer clear if the process itself seems too intimidating. As one author rightly notes:

> A number of studies have shown that the way people join an organization greatly influences how they function in that organization after joining. This is true of joining a church as well. The manner in which people join your church will determine their effectiveness as members for years to come.[1]

You need to have a clear, simple way of getting people plugged into the next step along the assimilation continuum—Membership Class.

As I have detailed, the Connection Card is the point of all communication at The Journey. This goes for expressing an interest in membership as well. Every week, the Next Steps on the unchanging portion of the Connection Card include a request for more information on membership. At any point, regular attenders can check that box and we will get them plugged into the next Membership Class. On the Sundays when we are teaching specifically on membership or when we plan to make a special point of it in a felt-need message, the Next Step option is emphasized. For example, we often schedule a specific Sunday to teach on membership when there is a Membership Class coming up. Then we reword the Next Step on the Connection Card to be even more pointed, such as: *Sign me up to attend the Membership Class on Sunday, March 12.*

As you will see in the next chapter, Membership Class is your opportunity to explain all of your church's requirements for membership, get any additional information from your prospective members, and embark on the membership journey. At this point, though, the only things your prospective members need to understand is (1) why they should join the church and (2) what they have to do to get plugged in. Give them a clear invitation to make the initial commitment by checking the Next Step box and showing up for class—the rest will follow.

4. Encourage membership through small groups.

I've already discussed the importance of small groups for helping people connect to your church and grow in their faith. In addition, small groups can be effective for encouraging regular attenders to take the step of membership. As regular attenders who are in a small group begin to form friendships with others and serve together with their group at the service (something we ask all groups to do several times each semester), they will begin to feel a strong sense of ownership. Not to mention, they will be rubbing shoulders each week with others in their group who are already members. Those two things work together to create a sense of positive peer pressure toward membership.

Stay aware of the regular attenders in your church who are not yet involved in a group. Do all you can to challenge them to get into one. When new groups are about to begin, consider sending a special email invitation to disconnected regular attenders and include a link to sign up online. Then, once those attenders are connected, do the following:

- Train your small group leaders to talk about membership and to encourage their group members who aren't yet members of the church to take that step.
- When you teach on membership, make a point of challenging those who are already taking ownership in the church—particularly as small group participants—to go ahead and take the step of membership.

Nothing can accelerate the growth of a regular attender more than taking part in the service on Sunday and being in a small group during the week. If those two things are happening in the life of your regular attenders, they are well on their way to being fully engaged members. (For detailed teaching on how to get 100 percent of your attenders involved in a small group, see my book *Activate: An Entirely New Approach to Small Groups*.)

The Problem of Meager Membership

Many churches today place little to no emphasis on asking people to join. Some theorists speculate that this lackadaisical attitude toward membership is the result of the modern church's come-as-you-are mentality. There is also an underlying fear of pushing membership on a culture reticent of joining anything. Too many churches think it is better to continually have the same nonmembers in attendance than to mention membership and risk scaring them away. This is a backward mind-set that undermines the power of the church body as established by Christ.

Church membership is not optional and should not be viewed as such. If you don't encourage your regular attenders to become members, you are doing them a disservice. In effect, you are stifling their spiritual development. The fear that leads to today's meager membership numbers is the enemy's newest way of keeping Christians disconnected from one another. As leaders, you and I have a responsibility to educate our attenders on the importance of being part of the church family and then to hold them to what they have learned. Membership allows us to hold people accountable for their spiritual walk in a way that keeps them on the track that leads to their becoming fully developing followers of Jesus Christ.

The Ultimate Goal

The heart—and the ultimate goal—of the Fusion assimilation system is to introduce new people to God and to help them become fully developing followers of Jesus. Salvation can happen at any point in the process. You and I are called to do our work with excellence so that the people sitting in our congregations will be more open to what God wants to do in them. As we partner with God in this process, he will draw people to himself in different ways and at different times during their assimilation journeys.

Someone may decide to trust Jesus as you extend an invitation in the weekly service and check the box on the back of the Connection Card indicating that he or she is making a first-time decision for Christ. Someone else may decide to take the step of salvation after a few weeks of serving alongside passionate Christians or after some time creating relationships with the roomful of believers in his or her small group. Another person may trust Jesus when you detail the plan of salvation at Membership Class (as we'll discuss in the next chapter).

Regardless of when each newcomer comes to faith, this is why all of the work you are putting in is worth it. Your assimilation process means nothing if it's not leading the people God sends you to step into the fullness of life that's only available through him. Again, only God can draw people into a relationship with him. That's his work and his alone— but he has asked you to help set the stage, to do your part to exemplify his character to those he has entrusted to you, to remove all stumbling blocks from their journey toward his truth . . . and then to help them grow as new disciples. What a joyous responsibility. (For a free copy of my new believer's guide, *The Next Step for Your Journey*, and other new believer resources, visit www.FusionBook.com.)

9

full circle

Every new beginning comes from some other beginning's end.

Seneca

Grow in the grace and knowledge of our Lord and Savior Jesus Christ. All glory to him, both now and forever!

Apostle Peter (2 Pet. 3:18)

Commencement is a word with double meaning. Strictly speaking, it is defined as a beginning. But all of us who have ever worked toward and waited for our own commencement ceremony know that it just as assuredly represents an end— an end to studying, an end to a known way of life, and the end of a specific set of goals and requirements. With this ending comes the promise of a new chapter, the beginning of the life we've been working toward.

Membership Class is the commencement ceremony for your assimilation process. It signals both an end and a beginning. When your regular attenders walk into Membership Class, they are taking their final steps of the assimilation journey. Their presence says, *I want to be a part of this family*, or *Hey, I am now assimilated!* You have guided them through the system, and thanks to the power of the Holy Spirit, they have come to the place of understanding their need to be joined with the body of Christ. That new person who showed up on your doorstep as a first-time guest mere months ago is now poised to be a vibrant, faithful member of your church family.

Jon looks around as he pulls into FCC's parking lot. All around him, people hurry through the cars toward the entrance. He sees his friend Brian—the one he met playing football in the park—greeting people at the door.

"Seems like yesterday that we drove into this parking lot for the first time," Jon says.

"It really does," answers Liz. "Remember the bad mood you were in that day?"

"I was not," Jon says and then pauses. "Well, okay, maybe a little. Any idea how long the Membership Class is going to last this afternoon?"

"They said about three hours. Why? Are you nervous about it?"

"No. But this is a big step," Jon answers. "I'm not nervous though. Everything in me says that it's the right thing to do."

Class Notes

Teaching Membership Class is one of my greatest joys as a pastor. Seeing God's faithfulness in bringing new followers into our congregations is a gift for assimilation-minded church leaders. When you can look back and know that you have thoughtfully steered your unchurched guests through the levels of the assimilation system, praying at each turn that you were effectively doing your part to facilitate their spiritual development, their decision to say yes to membership is exhilarating.

You have watched and nurtured them as they have discovered God working in their lives. You have used the system while trusting the Spirit. And when class day comes, you have an incredible opportunity to taste the fruit of your willingness to prepare the way. What's better than seeing people who were, when they first came to you, searching for answers decide to commit themselves to Jesus Christ and his church?

I also love teaching Membership Class because it provides an incredible opportunity to shape what kind of members I will have. As we discussed in the last chapter, the way a person joins an organization generally indicates the way that person will participate in the organization. If you make the class strong, it will produce strong, dedicated members. Your Fusion assimilation system's commencement ceremony marks the beginning of your attenders' newfound membership in the congregation. Generally this is where their deepest spiritual growth will begin to take place, thanks to the involvement level, spiritual disciplines, and accountability guidelines that you will be responsible for holding them to as members.

That being said, Membership Class is simply the doorway through which your attenders become connected with the church so that deeper spiritual development can begin. This is not the time to delve into material on the Beatitudes or about maintaining Christian disciplines. Instead, take advantage of your class time to explain the new relationship that membership signifies. Detail the rights and requirements of membership to those joining your congregation. Emphasize the philosophy and vision of your church. Underscore the commitment your members are entering into, and ensure that each and every prospective member is spiritually ready to move forward. Build the foundation carefully and you will welcome new members who are excited about partnering with you in ministry.

In *The Purpose-Driven Church*, Rick Warren suggests nine questions to focus on in your Membership Class:

1. What is a church?
2. What are the purposes of the church?
3. What are the benefits of being a member?
4. What are the requirements for membership?
5. What are the responsibilities of membership?
6. What is the vision and strategy of this church?
7. How is the church organized?
8. How can I get involved in ministry?
9. What do I do now that I am a member?[1]

At The Journey, we offer Membership Class every other month. It is a three-hour commitment on a Sunday afternoon.

Our goal is to answer the questions listed on the previous page and to signify every new member's commitment by having him or her sign a Membership Covenant. (See appendix C for a sample class schedule and for the covenant used at The Journey. Visit www.FusionBook.com for a downloadable covenant.)

As mentioned in the previous chapter, the Connection Card is our point of communication with those interested in attending. In the weeks preceding the class, our card will feature a Next Step that reads: *Sign me up for Membership Class on Sunday, [date]*. Prospective members simply check that box, and we follow up with them to ensure their attendance. On class day, we convene in the afternoon just after our last morning service so that those planning to attend can come to the late worship service and stay for class. We provide a quick, light lunch and then get down to business.

When you are discussing the requirements for membership, be sure to let your prospective members know that faith in Christ tops the list. (See appendix C for a list of The Journey's requirements for membership.) Hopefully during the period between their first visit and the day of Membership Class, all of your attenders will have made a profession of faith in Jesus. But just in case some of them haven't yet made that commitment, you should provide another opportunity. If you take the time in Membership Class to present the gospel and give an invitation, many will follow Christ. This is a time when their hearts are tender toward God. He is drawing them or they would not be in the class. Don't miss the opportunity to invite them into relationship with him before welcoming them to membership—only then will their assimilation journey be truly complete.

As Tim finishes outlining the vision for FCC's future outreach, Jon and Liz exchange impressed glances. Still, Jon can't shake an uneasy feeling that something is not quite right with all of this. Over the last few weeks, he has heard Tim and the other pastors talk about a personal relationship with God, but Jon has always forced himself to tune out. That's the part that doesn't quite make sense to him—or does it?

"Now let's talk about the requirements for membership here at FCC," Tim says from the front of the room. "The first and most important requirement is that you are a Christian—that you have come to a point in your life where you have acknowledged your need for Christ and accepted him as your personal Savior. In Romans, Paul tells us that . . ."

As Tim continues to speak, Jon finds himself listening more intently than ever before. For some strange reason, he feels as if Tim is speaking directly to him. His hands start to sweat a little. He looks over at Liz to see if she is feeling this, too. Her eyes are locked on Tim.

"If there is anyone in this class today who has not yet accepted Christ, I want to invite you to do so right now. You wouldn't be sitting here, seeking out information on joining this church, if Jesus had not been calling you to himself. Before you take the step to become a member of his family, you must say yes to him on a personal level. If I am talking to you, bow your head and pray this prayer with me . . ."

Jon bows his head and squints his eyes closed, his heart thumping loudly in his ears. Every word that Tim prays, Jon repeats silently to God. Liz's hand finds his with a squeeze.

He intertwines his fingers with hers, lets out a deep breath, and continues to pray.

Evangelism to Assimilation and Back Again

Again, the heart of the Fusion assimilation system is to introduce new people to God and help them become fully developing followers of Jesus Christ. That's it. Church membership is not about numbers for numbers' sake. Rather, it's a measurement of how well your attenders are developing spiritually. If they aren't aware of their need to belong, they are stunted in their spiritual growth. If they don't understand their place in the body, they lack discernment about God's intention for their lives. When attenders cross the line to membership, you have amplified permission to disciple them on a deeper level and hold them accountable for continuing to seek after God's best.

As such, the most important requirement for membership is a personal relationship with Jesus Christ. In your Membership Class, take the time to detail the plan of salvation for your prospective members and invite anyone who hasn't already done so to trust in Jesus. Most of those in attendance will have already accepted Jesus at some point during the assimilation process. Those who may still be unsure about their salvation will likely take that step when you give them the opportunity during the class. If there's anyone in the Membership Class who wants to join your church but isn't ready to say *yes* to a relationship with Christ, gently encourage that person to spend some more time getting connected in other ways and seeking God before taking the step of membership.

Once your newcomers are official members who are continually working toward becoming fully developing followers of Jesus, they are the voice in the world for his church. This is how the assimilation system comes full circle. An assimilated member is someone who will, inevitably, turn back toward evangelism. That evangelism continues the flow of first-time guests into your congregation each and every week. As the spiral winds, your new first-time guests become regular attenders and then members who, in various ways, invite more first-time guests into your congregation. Your assimilation system will be spinning constantly—and God will be working through it to continually draw new people to himself.

It's Friday afternoon. Kevin checks the clock on his desk, willing the hour hand to move faster. He can't wait for the weekend ahead. He's got no real plans except to make his world-famous chili and watch some football on Sunday. He's about to jump online to check the matchups and schedule when Jon knocks on his door. Oh no. Jon has been trying to get him to visit his church for a couple of months now, and Kevin is starting to run out of excuses. Before Kevin knows what's happened, he has promised away his Sunday morning.

conclusion

Have a bias toward action—let's see something happen now. You can break that big plan into small steps and take the first step right away.

Gandhi

To those who use well what they are given, even more will be given. . . . But from those who do nothing, even what little they have will be taken away.

Jesus (Matt. 25:29)

For over half a century, the Billy Graham organization has been introducing new believers to the Good News of Jesus. During his years of ministry, Dr. Graham acted as pastor to presidents and average Joes alike. He shared the truth of the gospel with more people than anyone else in the history of the church. In the process, he not only proved his complete dependence on God, but also his understanding of the spiritual principles that are at work all around us. When organizing his famed crusades, Dr. Graham never underestimated what I call *The Principle of Spiritual Readiness*. Instead, he embraced its power and worked with it in order to clear the pathway for as many people as possible to step toward Jesus.

Thanks to *The Principle of Spiritual Readiness*, Dr. Graham's crusade teams have been able to predict, with incredible accuracy, the number of people who will accept the invitation to leave their seats and step into life change. How do they know in advance how many hearts God will prompt? Of course, they can never know exactly—and they would never claim to—but they do understand and utilize this biblical truth: God will never give you more than you are prepared to receive. They understand that the number of people who will come forward corresponds directly to the number of volunteers they have in place to receive them. God works in conjunction with our level of readiness. And why shouldn't he? Why would he entrust us with more people than we are prepared to handle? And if God won't outpace the Billy Graham Evangelistic Association's level of readiness, he sure won't outpace yours and mine.

At The Journey, we make it a habit to always have more resources in place than we think we are going to need. For example, if we are starting a new series and giving away a free book, we have at least 20 percent more books on hand than may seem rational. Why? Because we want to make sure that we have done our part to be prepared for any surplus that God may decide to send us. I don't want to be the stumbling block if he's ready to bless us with more guests. I always try to ask myself: *If God sent us twice as many first-time guests as usual this week, would we be ready for them?* Thanks to the Fusion assimilation system, which flows largely from *The Principle of Spiritual Readiness*, I can honestly answer yes on a consistent basis—and if you apply what we've learned in these pages, you will be able to, too.

The System

Let's take a moment to recap: as we've seen, the Fusion assimilation system is built around a three-step process that leads your guests from their initial visit to their participation in Membership Class, with the intention of seeing them become fully developing followers of Jesus. You now have the blueprint and the tools you need to build the bridge for their journey. The first step—your first goal—is to turn them from first-time guests into second-time guests:

- Make a stellar first impression with your pre-service by ensuring that guests are properly *greeted*, *directed*, *treated*, and *seated*.
- Encourage guests to complete a Connection Card and drop it in the offering so they can receive their free gift.
- Follow up in a *fast*, *friendly*, and *functional* way, through an email within thirty-six hours and a handwritten note with a small gift within ninety-six hours of the initial visit.

When your first-time guests return for a second visit, your assimilation system is working! They are asking to walk a little farther across the bridge. Your goal now is to turn them from second-time guests into regular attenders:

- Re-create the pre-service they are expecting, thanks to the Fusion assimilation system's ubiquity.
- Encourage them to complete a Connection Card to let you know that they are second-time guests and urge them toward deeper involvement by suggesting some Next Steps.
- Follow up in a *fast*, *friendly*, and *functional* way, through an email within thirty-six hours and a typed letter with a small gift within ninety-six hours of their visit—both suggesting additional Next Steps and more ways for them to get plugged in.

After your guests have visited a second time, your goal is to keep them on the journey by turning them into members:

- Encourage them to get involved in sticky situations where they will form connections and friendships with other people. The four most effective sticky situations are small groups, fun events, service teams, and newcomer receptions.
- Encourage them to take on *responsibility* within the church, which will lead to a sense of *ownership*.
- Encourage membership through multiplying service opportunities, teaching, regular sign-ups, and small groups.
- Hold a regular Membership Class, where you ensure that they have accepted Jesus and discuss the details of joining your church.

When you start intentionally preparing yourself to receive first-time guests, with a heart bent on prayer and an eye set on excellence, you will start receiving them. The

Fusion assimilation system gives you the ability to fulfill your responsibility in this partnership with God. He has called you to step up and graciously accept the gifts he wants to send your way by doing all you can to represent his kingdom well.

The Fusion assimilation system is a tool. Trust the Spirit, use the system—and use it consistently. It will take about six months for you to start seeing visible growth results, so don't get discouraged. You have to sow before you can reap. Systems for accomplishing God's work have been implemented since biblical times, and God has continually worked through them with amazing results. Experience has shown us that he now stands ready to work through this system as you take steps to put it in place.

In the first chapter, we learned that you have to know where you are before you can get where you want to go. So now that we have come full circle, do you know where you are? How are those numbers looking? How is your current assimilation process working for you? Have you started implementing concepts of the system as you have been reading? Are you ready to really get going? Where should you begin?

Take Action

Gandhi once said, "Have a bias toward action—let's see something happen now. You can break that big plan into small steps and take the first step right away." Taking on a new way of doing things—a new plan—can be intimidating, I know. Let me encourage you to take Gandhi's advice. Break the Fusion system into small steps and take the first step right away. You know the first goal: to earn a return visit from your first-time guest. So start doing something to accomplish that goal. Even if you need to start small and build toward implementing the full system, you will see results from your efforts. A series of small steps repeated over and over again will reap big rewards—eternal rewards—when your focus is on changing lives. Here are seven small things you can do to get started right away:

1. Buy some note cards and start handwriting follow-up notes for your first-timers.
2. Change your Connection Card to ask for only relevant information.
3. Put up signs to direct people toward your bathrooms, children's area, and so forth.
4. Take a hard look at your building—cut the grass, pick up clutter, paint a sign.
5. Start offering generous, enticing refreshments.
6. Position smiling, friendly greeters at your front door.
7. Put together an assimilation volunteer team and study this book together.

Just take action. Jump in. You don't have to be ready to put the entire system in place. When you start to consistently take small steps that make your first-timers feel welcome and encourage them to come back, your efforts will pay off for your second-timers, regular attenders, and members as well. Your people will start noticing a shift in attitude. They will see a renewed intention toward doing things with excellence. And excellence begets excellence. You won't be able to stop the positive results.

On the other hand, if you don't decide to act now, you will continue to be acted upon by outside forces—forces like comfort and complacency—which lead to limited growth. As Stephen Covey writes in *The Seven Habits of Highly Effective People*:

> The difference between people who exercise initiative and those who don't is literally the difference between night and day. I'm not talking about a 25 to 50 percent difference in effectiveness; I'm talking about a 5,000-plus percent difference, particularly if they are smart, aware and sensitive to others. . . . If you wait to be acted upon, you will be acted upon. And growth and opportunity consequences attend either road.[1]

Likewise, churches that exercise assimilation initiative are far more effective in moving people toward becoming fully developing followers of Jesus. Think about it: you are saying something to your first-time guests already. What are they hearing? Either you are letting the forces of mediocrity cause you to convey indifference, or you are exercising some initiative to make their experience memorable.

You may already have some of what we've talked about in place and just need to support it with the bigger system and a focus on consistent excellence. Too many church leaders fail to do their part in this area. Your interest in the Fusion assimilation system proves that you are not one of those leaders. You understand that if God has called you to be a pastor, he has made you responsible for clearing the path toward knowing him more intimately—not just for those who are already in your congregation, but also for everyone who walks through your front door.

The Design of Transformation

Assimilation is not the only system that can help your church grow. Like the human body, the church is made up of a network of systems that work together to produce optimal health. There's the evangelism system, the worship-planning system, the ministry system, the small group system, the strategic system, the stewardship system, the leadership system, and, of course, the assimilation system. But of the eight systems, the assimilation system is the one that can most easily stand on its own. The other systems are more intricately intertwined. For example, if you are going to start a new stewardship strategy or a new small group strategy, other systems within your church are going to have to change as well. But you can develop and maintain a strong assimilation system without having to change any other area of your church. (For more details on each of these eight systems, including a free sixty-minute audio overview and the free ebook *Healthy Systems, Healthy Church*, visit www.FusionBook.com.)

Make a decision to start with one manageable thing.

If you decide to make improvements in the way you assimilate newcomers, you will see growth. Period. By taking on this one system, you can increase the number of people who stick with you long enough for you to make a difference in their lives. And adhering to the Fusion assimilation system is something any church can do. As I travel around the country, teaching and implementing the concepts we have explored here together, I am amazed by the stories of people who have seen incredible growth by doing nothing but changing the way they handle first-time guests.

Now, a rising tide does raise all ships. Once you start this process, you may want to change some other things. Just imagine that you change your system of assimilation and, as you find yourself keeping more people, you start reaching out with stronger evangelism and then start stepping up your weekly services and small groups. Your church would suddenly become more effective than ever because you acted on a decision to stop taking your first-time guests for granted.

Make a decision to start with one manageable thing. Look at one thing you can do better this week—then do it. Look at one area you can change—then change it. Soon you will be looking at this one system in its entirety and the difference it can help you make in the life of one guest who walks through your door, and then the difference it can help you make in the life of the next guest who walks through your door, and the next one, and the next one. That's how the kingdom grows—one person at a time.

I will be praying for you as you work to build the bridge of assimilation in your church. We are all in this together, striving toward a common goal. I encourage you to share what you have learned with another church leader who may benefit from understanding the powerful role assimilation plays in opening people's hearts and minds. As Jesus calls new people to himself, may we do all we can to facilitate their journey.

> Let us not become weary in doing good, for at the proper time we will reap a harvest if we do not give up. (Apostle Paul, Gal. 6:9 NIV)

postscript

I hope this book will become a conversation starter between you and me. My team and I are constantly developing resources and gathering ideas to help you keep first-time guests and move them toward membership. We would love to hear your story and discuss ways we can grow together for God's glory. Please contact us at this book's website:

www.FusionBook.com

When you visit www.FusionBook.com, you will also find free resources to assist you in implementing the principles of this book, relevant podcasts, and a ton of additional up-to-date articles and tips.

Your partner in ministry,

Nelson Searcy

appendix a

the fusion assimilation system

Assimilation System Outline

First-Time Visit

- A person attends a service for the first time and fills out a Connection Card.

- Following the service, the first-time guest receives a free book and can visit the guest table to ask questions or talk with a volunteer or staff person.

- The guest receives an email within thirty-six hours of attending a service. This email includes a link to an online survey that encourages feedback from the first visit and connects the person to the church's website.

- The guest receives a handwritten note in the mail within ninety-six hours of attending a service. In addition to a postcard describing the current message series, this note includes an unexpected gift to *wow* the first-time guest. The gift is relevant to the target demographic.

- The guest receives a typed letter in the mail approximately one month after the first visit. Included in the letter are another gift and an audio message from a prior service.

Second-Time Visit

- A person attends a service for the second time and again fills out a Connection Card.

- The person receives an email within thirty-six hours of the second visit. This email focuses on a specific way the person can get connected at the church.

- The person receives a typed letter in the mail within ninety-six hours of the second visit. Included in the letter is a second surprise gift that someone in the target demographic would appreciate.

Regular Attender

- A regular attender is encouraged to sign up for volunteer teams, fun events, small groups, baptism, and Membership Class on a weekly basis.

- The regular attender is eligible to attend Membership Class after attending the church regularly for two months.

The Assimilation Process

Mission (Example—The Journey Church)

The Journey exists to give the people of New York City the best opportunity to become fully developing followers of Jesus.

As a part of this overall mission, The Journey's assimilation system exists to move people forward along a three-step process:

1. From being first-time guests to becoming second-time guests
2. From being second-time guests to becoming regular attenders
3. From being regular attenders to becoming fully developing members

Assumption

This strategy is based on the assumption that once people become fully engaged members (people working out the five purposes in their life at The Journey—see below), they are experiencing real life transformation and as a result are in the process of becoming fully developing followers of Jesus (the ultimate mission of the church).

The five purposes members work out in their lives are (1) accepting the invitation to an intimate relationship with

God, (2) connecting to healthy relationships with other Christians, (3) moving toward an authentic commitment to God, (4) becoming involved in life-changing ministry and mission in the city and the world, and (5) honoring God completely.

Goal

The goal of assimilation at The Journey is to move people to take the important and life-changing step of church membership.

appendix b

assimilation tools

Connection Card—Front

COMMUNICATION CARD		January 8, 2006

Dr. / Mr. / Mrs. / Ms.
Name: _____ O Change in contact information

Email (please print): _____

O 1st-time guest	Address: _____ Apt. _____
O 2nd-time guest	City: _____ State _____ Zip _____
O Regular Attender	Best Contact Phone: (____) _____
O Member	

If 1st- or 2nd-time guest, how did you hear about The Journey? _____
(Name of person who invited you, postcard, mailer, newspaper)

Place this card in the offering when it is given or hand it in at the Case for Faith table as you leave.

Connection Card—Back

MY NEXT STEP TODAY IS TO:	**SEND ME INFO ABOUT:**
O Memorize Proverbs 7:2–3.	O Becoming a follower of Jesus.
O Read the story of Solomon in 1 Kings 3.	O Baptism.
O Accept the One-Year Bible Challenge.	O Growth Groups.
O Find out more about upcoming Play Groups:	O Church membership.
O Friday, Jan. 20: Glory Road Movie Play Group	O Serving @ The Journey.
O Friday, Jan. 27: Extreme Bowling	O Servant Evangelism Saturday.

Sign me up for Growth Group # _____

Comments, Prayer Requests: _____
_____
_____

First-Time Guest 36-Hour Email Response (Pages 96–97)

Subject: Great to see you at The Journey!

From: [Your name (or name of the pastor who taught on Sunday, if not you)]

Hey [first name],

I had an open moment this morning and I wanted to shoot you a quick email to let you know it was great to have you at The Journey on Sunday—hope your first experience was meaningful and enjoyable.

Would you do me a favor?

Because it's important to us that you felt welcomed and had a positive experience your first time at The Journey, would you take a few seconds to fill out a quick online survey for me? (It will only take about thirty seconds.)

[web address]

Or just reply to this email and let me know your thoughts.

If there is anything I can do for you, or if there is a specific way that I can be praying for you . . . please feel free to let me know.

I'll be in touch again soon.

[your name]

P.S. I've attached a picture of my family, and here are a few bits of info:

1. My name is [first name], and my wife's name is [first name]. We have been married for [number] years!

2. We have a son named [first name] (born in [year])—you'll see him running around Journey Kidz on Sundays.

3. My wife and I are longtime bulldog owners, but we are currently "in between," so our house is currently dog hair–free.

4. Before moving here, I pastored on the Upper West Side of Manhattan for ten years. I'm still looking for a great NYC cheesecake around here. Let me know if you have a recommendation!

———

[your name]

[your title, church name]

[web address]

Check out The Journey on Facebook:

[web address]

First-Time and Second-Time Guest Online Survey (Page 96)

To view my current first- and second-time guest surveys, visit www.FusionBook.com.

First-Time Guest 96-Hour Snail-Mail Response (Pages 101–2)

Hi [guest's name],

Great to see you on Sunday at The Journey. We hope your time with us was both meaningful and relevant to your life—and that you had a good time, too!

Enclosed is a five-dollar MetroCard, good on all NYC subways and buses . . . so take a Journey on us! We hope to see you again soon. Hope you have a great week.

God bless,
[your name]
[your title, church name]
[your email address]

One-Month Follow-Up Letter (Pages 105–7)

[Date]

Hi [first name],

It's hard to believe that it has been thirty days since your first visit!

We hope that you found The Journey to be a welcoming, relevant, and fun place to get plugged in and meet other people. We also hope you found The Journey to be a place where you could encounter God and have a meaningful worship experience.

To celebrate your one-month anniversary with The Journey, we have a gift that we hope helps you grow closer to God. It's a CD of a message we taught called "Getting Fit Spiritually." We pray you find it to be relevant to your own personal journey.

I also want to encourage you to get connected to a Growth Group this summer!

One of the best ways to meet new people and grow in your faith at The Journey is to sign up for a Growth Group.

Growth Groups are The Journey's groups of fifteen or so people who get together each week (Summer Growth Groups begin in June and last through August) in a convenient metro New York City location to grow and have fun together.

Sign-ups for our Summer Growth Groups have just started . . . and there are over sixty great groups to choose from. So . . . NOW is the perfect time to sign up!

You can sign up for a Summer Growth Group at any Journey service this Sunday or online TODAY at this link:

[web address]

Please let us know if there is any way that we can be praying for you. Have a wonderful week, and we look forward to seeing you again soon @ The Journey!

On the journey together . . .

[your signature]
[your title, church name]
[your email address]

P.S.—Don't miss this Sunday as we begin our new teaching series "Train to Win: Developing the Core Strengths of the Christian Faith," with the message "Personal God." See you there!

36-Hour Second-Time Email Response (Page 118)

Subject: Glad to have you back at The Journey!

From: [Your name (or name of the pastor who taught on Sunday, if not you)]

Hi [guest's name],

I'm glad that you were able to join us again Sunday at The Journey. It's good to know that we did not scare you off after your first time with us :-). I hope you enjoyed your second time as we talked about "Friendship: Wireless Connections."

There are a lot of easy ways to get plugged in at The Journey. If you have not already, you can sign up for the Growth Group of your choice on any Sunday or during the week anytime on our website [link]. I hope you decide to get plugged into one of our small groups.

We would love for you to take thirty seconds to fill out one more survey for us. Just click here or visit our website [link] and let us know how you felt about your second visit to The Journey. We want to know your thoughts so that we can serve you better.

I will be praying for you this week. If there is anything specific that we can be praying for you about, if you have any questions, or if there is anything we can do for you this week, please don't hesitate to let me know.

Have a great week and God bless,

[your name]

[your title, church name]

P.S. Don't forget: This weekend we continue our series "Life 360" at The Journey. You don't want to miss it! Invite a friend, too. I look forward to seeing you then.

96-Hour Second-Time Snail-Mail Response (Pages 120–21)

[Date]

Hi [First name],

It was great to see you again at The Journey on Sunday. We're excited that you chose to check out The Journey a second time! To show our appreciation, we have enclosed a Starbucks card for a free beverage on us. We hope you enjoy it.

I also want to encourage you to get connected to a **Growth Group this summer!**

One of the best ways to meet new people and grow in your faith at The Journey is to sign up for a Growth Group. Growth Groups are The Journey's groups of fifteen or so people who get together each week (Summer Growth Groups begin in June and last through August) in a convenient metro New York City location to grow and have fun together.

Sign-ups for our Summer Growth Groups have just started . . . and there are over sixty great groups to choose from. So . . . NOW is the perfect time to sign up!

You can sign up for a Summer Growth Group at any Journey service this Sunday or online TODAY at this link:

[web address]

Please let us know if there is anything we can do for you or if there is a specific way that we can be praying for you this week.

We look forward to seeing you this Sunday. Have a great week, and God bless!

On the journey . . .

> *[your signature]*
> *[your name]*
> *[your title, church name]*
> *[your email address]*

P.S. Don't forget: This weekend we continue "Life 360" by examining how we can have a high-definition faith. You will not want to miss it! Invite a friend to come with you. We look forward to seeing you then.

First Response Team Follow-Up Checklist

Please check and initial each item after completion.

First-Time Guests

☐ _____ Write a note card with the message from Sunday's teaching pastor.

☐ _____ Print out list of first-time guests. For each guest, fill out the name on the card and address an envelope.

☐ _____ Place the note card, free gift, and a series-specific info card into the envelope.

☐ _____ Put a return address label over the back of the envelope and a stamp in the right-hand corner.

☐ _____ Mail immediately.

Second-Time Guests

☐ _____ Print out list of second-time guests.

☐ _____ Print a letter to each guest, placing his or her name after the word *Hi* in the salutation.

☐ _____ Address a regular letter envelope for each guest with an address (check the list beforehand to obtain the address if it is not on the list). Place a stamp and a return address label on the envelope.

☐ _____ Place the letter and a gift card into the envelope and mail immediately.

One-Month Follow-Up

☐ _____ Obtain the names and addresses of first-time guests from the previous month, closest to the week you are currently in (e.g., second week, third week).

☐ _____ Create mailing labels for the envelopes in Word, using the Excel database to do a mail merge, then print the mailing labels (size 5160).

☐ _____ Address a letter (written by the lead pastor) to each person listed with an address (again, you might need to check the mailing list beforehand to obtain addresses not on the list).

☐ _____ Place a message CD or DVD (already prepared and determined by the pastors), a series-specific info card, and the letter in an envelope. Make sure the name of the addressee matches the greeting of the letter.

☐ _____ Mail immediately.

Remember:

Each time we contact a person we are showing the love of Christ. Jesus says that the Father wills that none should be lost: "What do you think? If a man owns a hundred sheep, and one of them wanders away, will he not leave the ninety-nine on the hills and go to look for the one that wandered off? . . . In the same way, your Father in heaven is not willing that any of these little ones should be lost" (Matt. 18:12, 14 NIV). Thank you for serving in this way!

appendix c

membership tools

Teaching the Necessity of a Spiritual Family

To move regular attenders down the road to membership, it's important to teach about the significance of participating in the body of Christ (see chapter 8 for more on this). Here are four primary reasons for membership you should regularly communicate to your congregation:

1. *You need healthy relationships.* "Two are better than one, because they have a good return for their work: If one falls down, his friend can help him up. But pity the one who falls and has no one to help him up!" (Eccles. 4:9–10 NIV).

2. *You need a place where you can use your gifts.* "Do not neglect the gift that is in you, which was given to you" (1 Tim. 4:14 NKJV).

3. *You need a place where you can grow.* "The believers devoted themselves to the apostles' teaching, and to fellowship, and to sharing meals (including the Lord's Supper), and to prayer" (Acts 2:42).
4. *You need to belong to something bigger than yourself.* "Just as each of us has one body with many members, and these members do not all have the same function, so in Christ we who are many form one body, and each member belongs to all the others" (Rom. 12:4–5 NIV). "Let us not give up meeting together, as some are in the habit of doing, but let us encourage one another" (Heb. 10:25 NIV).

Service Opportunity Job Descriptions

Growing responsibility is a key component in fostering a sense of ownership among regular attenders. Here are a few of the job descriptions we use for people who serve at The Journey:

Greeter

By serving as a greeter today, you have the opportunity to make The Journey's first impression on our guests. Many times people make a decision about a church based on their first impressions. One of the core values at The Journey is to create an authentic and nonthreatening environment. You have the opportunity to convey that from the moment people walk in the door! Smile warmly, distribute programs, and let each person know that we're glad they are here.

Hospitality Host

By serving as a hospitality host today, you have the opportunity to make The Journey's first impression on our guests. We want to make our guests (and regular attenders) feel welcome every Sunday! A hospitality host goes one step further than the greeter and seeks to make connections with our first-time guests, answer questions, and make them feel welcome. Be on the lookout for anyone who appears unsure about where to go. Help them find what they're looking for by providing a personal escort. Let them know they're important!

Resource Team

By serving on the Resource Team, you have the opportunity to share with other people about the different ministries at The Journey. By sharing with people in the church about our ministries and resources, you play a part in helping them get plugged into ministry.

Usher

By serving as an usher today, you have the opportunity to help people feel comfortable at The Journey. Many times people make a decision about a church based on their first impressions. One of the core values at The Journey is to create an authentic and nonthreatening environment. You have the opportunity to convey that by smoothing the way for people to participate in the service. Escort people to open seats and make sure they are comfortable where they have been seated—and smile!

Membership Class Follow-Up Email

When regular attenders indicate their interest in pursuing membership on their Connection Card, we follow up with an email like this one:

Hi [first name],

Thank you for expressing interest in membership at The Journey. I'm excited that you are considering making The Journey your spiritual family!

The Journey's next Membership Class is coming up on Sunday, [date], from 3:30 to 6:30 p.m., and we would love for you to be a part. There is only one requirement for attending Membership Class: By [date of the Membership Class], you need to have been attending The Journey for two months. If you meet that requirement, you are qualified to attend Membership Class. If not, we have upcoming classes on Sunday, November 7, and Sunday, December 5, and we'll look forward to you joining us then!

By attending Membership Class, you are not making the commitment to become a member (though you will have the option to become a member at the end of the class). Membership Class is an opportunity for you to explore membership at The Journey, to find out more about The Journey, and to ask any questions that you might have.

All you have to do is reply to this email and let me know whether or not you are planning to attend Membership Class on Sunday, [date]. It is important that you RSVP for this class, so I look forward to hearing from you soon.

Thanks again, and I will be praying for you as you consider taking this important step.

God bless,

Pastor Nelson

The Journey Membership Class Schedule

3:30 p.m.   Arrival/pictures

3:40 p.m.   Welcome/introductions/complete membership info sheet

4:05 p.m.   Introduction to Membership Class

4:10 p.m.   Timeline and history of The Journey (video with Nelson Searcy)

4:25 p.m.   Why join The Journey?

4:35 p.m.   The Journey Membership Requirements
One-Verse Evangelism video
Baptism video (after baptism section)

4:55 p.m.   Purpose of The Journey
Purpose Statement video

5:15 p.m.   Core Values of The Journey

5:30 p.m.   Affiliation and Sponsors of The Journey
Next Step: Pray for those in your Membership Class

5:35 p.m.   BREAK
Class photo
Humorous video clip (coming back from the break)

5:50 p.m.   The Structure of The Journey

6:10 p.m.   Membership Expectations

6:25 p.m.   The Unchurched and The Journey

6:30 p.m.   The Journey Membership Covenant
Complete application
Sign Membership Covenant
Depart for servant evangelism project

The Journey Membership Requirements

1. *Salvation*—The person must have a personal relationship with Jesus Christ.
2. *Baptism*—The adult believer is immersed in water.
3. *Attendance*—The person must have faithfully attended The Journey for two months.

The Journey Membership Covenant

1. **I will protect the unity of my church** by acting in love toward other members, by refusing to gossip, and by following the leaders.
2. **I will share the responsibility of my church** by praying for its growth, by inviting the unchurched to attend, and by warmly welcoming those who visit.
3. **I will serve the ministry of my church** by discovering my gifts and talents, by being equipped to serve by my pastors, and by developing a servant's heart.
4. **I will support the testimony of my church** by attending faithfully, by living a godly life, and by giving regularly.

Signature _____

Date _____

Baptism Follow-Up Email

When people indicate their interest in being baptized on their Connection Card, we follow up with an email like this:

Hi [first name],

Thank you for expressing interest in being baptized at The Journey. The Journey's next baptism is on Sunday afternoon, [date].

The baptism will be held from 1:30 to 2:30 p.m. at First Baptist Church located on the northwest corner of 79th Street and Broadway. It is only a short three-block walk from The Journey's Upper West Side location.

If you have any questions, feel free to let me know. You can also read more on what the Bible says about baptism and about The Journey's beliefs on baptism at [web address].

If you have begun a relationship with Jesus, I would love for you to participate in this very special celebration of baptism. All you need to do right now is respond to this email as soon as possible and let me know whether or not you are planning to join us on [date].

I look forward to hearing from you and hope you can participate with us on [date]. Have a wonderful week!

Blessings,

Pastor Nelson

appendix d

resources

Recommended Books and Resources by Nelson Searcy

Activate: An Entirely New Approach to Small Groups

Connect: How to Double Your Number of Volunteers

The Difference Maker: Using Your Everyday Life for Eternal Impact

Engage: A Guide to Creating Life-Transforming Worship Services

The Generosity Ladder: Your Next Step to Financial Peace

The Greatness Principle: Finding Significance and Joy by Serving Others

The Healthy Renegade Pastor: Abandoning Average in Your Health and Wellness

Ignite: How to Spark Immediate Growth in Your Church

Maximize: How to Develop Extravagant Givers in Your Church

The Renegade Pastor: Abandoning Average in Your Life and Ministry

Revolve: A New Way to See Worship

Tongue Pierced: How the Words You Speak Transform the Life You Live

Unshakable: Standing Strong When Things Go Wrong

CDs and Downloadable MP3s

The Assimilation Seminar—From First-Time Guests to Long-Time Members. Three-DVD set includes live recording of seminar and a resource CD.

Developing a One-Year Personal Growth Calendar. CD or MP3.

The Evangelism Seminar. Three-disc set includes live recording of seminar and a resource CD.

Fasting for Spiritual Breakthrough. CD or MP3.

The Leadership Skills for a Growing Church Seminar. CD.

Planning a One-Year Preaching Calendar. CD or MP3.

Reaching Your Community through Servant Evangelism. CD or MP3.

The Small-Groups Seminar. Three-disc set includes live recording of seminar and a resource CD.

Starting a Second Service. CD or MP3.

Starting Worship Arts from Scratch. CD or MP3.

The Stewardship Seminar. Three-disc set includes live recording of seminar and a resource CD.

The Strategy Seminar. Three-disc set includes live recording of seminar and a resource CD.

These and other resources are available at www.Church LeaderInsights.com.

notes

Chapter 1 The Power of Assimilation

1. Rick Warren, *The Purpose-Driven Church: Growth without Compromising Your Message and Mission* (Grand Rapids: Zondervan, 1995), 130–31.

Chapter 3 Seven Minutes and Counting

1. Timothy D. Wilson, *Strangers to Ourselves: Discovering the Adaptive Unconscious* (Cambridge, MA: Harvard University Press, 2002), 18.

2. Paul Ekman, quoted by Carlin Flora, "The Once-Over," *Psychology Today*, May/June 2004, http://psychologytoday.com/articles/pto-20040713-000 004.html.

3. Ken Blanchard, *Raving Fans: A Revolutionary Approach to Customer Service* (New York: William Morrow, 1993), 100.

4. Ibid., 102–3.

5. James Beard, *Beard on Food* (New York: Bloomsbury USA, 2007), xi.

Chapter 4 Making Contact

1. Dale Carnegie, *How to Win Friends and Influence People* (New York: Pocket Books/ Simon & Schuster, 1981), 246.

Chapter 7 Sticky Situations

1. Henry Cloud and John Townsend, *How People Grow: What the Bible Reveals about Personal Growth* (Grand Rapids: Zondervan, 2001), 122–23.

Chapter 8 Taking Ownership

1. Warren, *The Purpose-Driven Church*, 315.

Chapter 9 Full Circle

1. Warren, *The Purpose-Driven Church*, 316–17.

Conclusion

1. Stephen R. Covey, *The Seven Habits of Highly Effective People: Powerful Lessons in Personal Change* (New York: Free Press/Simon & Schuster, 2004), 76.

Nelson Searcy is the founding and lead pastor of The Journey Church. Started in 2002 in New York City, this groundbreaking church sees the majority of its growth coming from new believers and currently meets in locations in Manhattan, Queens, and Staten Island, as well as additional locations in San Francisco and Boca Raton. Nelson is the recipient of the prestigious 2013 Donald A. McGavran Award for Outstanding Leadership in Great Commission Research. He is the author of more than seventy-five church growth resources and twelve books, including *The Generosity Ladder*, *Maximize*, *Connect*, and *Ignite*. Nelson is also an experienced church planter, coach, and church-growth strategist. Before founding The Journey, he served as the director of the Purpose Driven Community at Saddleback Church. He is also the founder of ChurchLeaderInsights.com and the Renegade Pastors Network.

More Church Resources from Nelson Searcy

Transform Lives through Church Experiences

Serving in the Church

Create a Culture of
Generosity and Giving